"From the humblest start as an app. Zealand, Dean has become one of the forces to be reckoned with on the international baking scene. His skill, enthusiasm and ambition have no boundaries."

Lauraine Jacobs, MNZM
Food columnist, NZ Listener; former president of NZGFW & IACP

"Baking is a science and Dean is a brilliant scientist. His understanding of how and why ingredients work together is truly remarkable. When you combine his baking genius and his business acumen, you get a formidable force in the world of food. But behind that steely determination is also a truly great person whom I am proud to call my friend."

Dame Julie Christie, DNZM

"I've witnessed at close quarters Dean going from strength to strength as a businessman and entrepreneur. Dean's ability to conceive and manage multiple businesses in numerous countries, while still managing to co-create with his team, is well worth celebrating."

Peter Gordon, ONZM
Chef, restaurateur, writer & fusion food pioneer

"In my 28 years as an entrepreneur, I would be hard-pressed to name another founder of an F&B concept with the uncanny ability to repeatedly create, execute and operationalise a winning concept. Dean demands an attitude of excellence from those around him, fostering in his businesses a culture where attention to detail matters. Save every penny you can; spend every pound that you must. Not a cent more and not a dollar less where it counts."

Andrew Kwan
CEO, Commonwealth Capital Group, Asia

DEAN BRETTSCHNEIDER

PASSION
IS MY
MAIN
INGREDIENT

To Al,
enjoy The small read
of my style s. life so
far.
Best
Dean

mc Marshall Cavendish
Editions

Published by Marshall Cavendish Editions
An imprint of Marshall Cavendish International

A member of the
Times Publishing Group

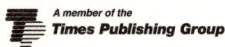

Other Marshall Cavendish Offices
Marshall Cavendish Corporation, 99 White Plains Road, Tarrytown NY 10591-9001,
USA • Marshall Cavendish International (Thailand) Co Ltd, 253 Asoke, 12th Flr,
Sukhumvit 21 Road, Klongtoey Nua, Wattana, Bangkok 10110, Thailand • Marshall
Cavendish (Malaysia) Sdn Bhd, Times Subang, Lot 46, Subang Hi-Tech Industrial
Park, Batu Tiga, 40000 Shah Alam, Selangor Darul Ehsan, Malaysia.

Marshall Cavendish is a registered trademark of Times Publishing Limited

National Library Board, Singapore Cataloguing in Publication Data

Name(s): Brettschneider, Dean.
Title: Passion is my main ingredient / Dean Brettschneider.
Description: Singapore : Marshall Cavendish Editions, 2019.
Identifier(s): OCN 1100468286 | ISBN 978-981-48-6801-3 (paperback)
Subject(s): LCSH: Brettschneider, Dean. | Bakers--Biography. | Bakeries.
Classification: DDC 338.761664752--dc23

Printed in Singapore

Cover photo by Claus Peuckert

Contents

One

The Basic Ingredients: The Beginnings

"'Brettschneider'? What kind of name is that?"

I've heard that a few too many times. I'll give you the short answer. The name has its origins from Gdansk, Poland, a city that sits right on the border with Germany. Our family tree is patchy, but we can trace it back to five generations ago, where we find a guy called Johannes Petrus Brettschneider, my great-great-grandfather. He was in the merchant navy in Gdansk and one day, for reasons known only to himself, he jumped on a boat and sailed to Amsterdam, where he promptly met and married a Dutch lady by the name of Willimeep (who, coincidentally, happened to make her living as a baker). So that's how the Brettschneider name arrived in Holland, which makes me Dutch, not German, as most people assume when they first hear my name.

Skip forward to World War II, when my father, Rudi, was a young boy being brought up in Amsterdam by his parents, Johannes and Elizabeth. Young Rudi survived to tell the tale of the war but my grandfather, unfortunately, did not. He died at only age 37. He didn't die fighting, but it was still the war that killed him. When fighting broke out, my grandfather escaped from a forced labour factory and went into hiding. He paid a sympathetic neighbour whatever little he could afford to let him stay in their attic. And that's where he remained, for years, as he waited out the war.

Little Rudi was only five years old at the time and desperately missed his father, too young to understand why he had to leave. When his crying became too much, Elizabeth would take the little boy to a park in front of the building where Johannes was hiding. From his perch in the attic, my opa would peer out at his wife and son from a narrow window, blowing kisses and hoping his tears weren't visible from such a distance.

The war ended and Johannes could finally come out of hiding, but when he did, he was frail and sick. He had developed cancer while in hiding and by the time the diagnosis came, it was much too late. The end came quickly. Naturally, Rudi blamed the war for his father's death and he grew to despise anything to do with the military. National military service was compulsory in Holland for all 18-year-old males at the time, and my father became determined to avoid it when his call-up came. He managed to dodge the draft for several years — using a variety of means that escalated in creativity and desperation — before he eventually ran out of excuses. Feeling like he had been backed into a corner, the then 20-year-old Rudi felt he had no choice but to leave. And so, he kissed his mum goodbye, sold the few possessions he had and hopped on a boat bound for New Zealand.

New Zealand wasn't a totally random destination for a young Dutchman. There has long been a connection and mutual fascination between the two places, stemming from the Dutch explorer Abel Tasman. He was the guy who first discovered Tasmania and New Zealand in the 1640s — the latter being named after the Dutch province of Zeeland. Strangely though, he rather absent-mindedly failed to claim New Zealand, allowing the old rogue Captain Cook to nip in and steal it for Great Britain.

My father was far from the only one treading the same path. Swathes of Europeans were emigrating to Australia and New Zealand in the 1960s. Many parts of Europe were still suffering the aftermath of the war, so these faraway islands held the promise of a new start. Still, it was a ballsy thing for a young guy to do. He barely spoke a word of English and he was practically penniless. I don't think he had much of a clue of what to expect on the other side.

After bouncing around a series of odd jobs for a while — from peeling potatoes to building bridges — my father ended up working at a sheep farm in Loburn, a small farming community in North Canterbury, about 30 minutes from Christchurch. Here he met the daughter of the Scottish family who owned the farm, his future wife of 48 years, Colleen Smith.

They married in 1966. My older brother, Hans, was born in 1968, followed by me a year after that. True to my future character, I arrived in a hurry. A few days premature and without much warning, I entered the world on the floor of my parents' living room, a frantic midwife having only made it with minutes to spare. When I tell people this, they often remark that it is no surprise I turned out the way I did, always pushing things forward and ensuring things get done, right this minute, no time for talking. The infant Dean couldn't even wait 30 minutes for his poor mother to get to the hospital.

By the time I was born, our family was living a stone's throw from Waikuku Beach on New Zealand's eastern coast, a few miles east of Loburn where my parents had first met. When I think of childhood memories, everything revolves around the outdoors. Waves, the beach, green fields, forests. I cycled everywhere — even the nearest town of Rangiora, where my nana lived, was three miles away — so I was always outside in the fresh air. And this being New Zealand, sport was part of the fabric of the place. I played rugby and cricket, of course, but also soccer, because of our Dutch roots. We had only one car so this invariably meant that whatever sports team one of us two brothers were part of, the other brother would be carted along too. After spending two hours on a car ride somewhere, I figured I might as well pull on a jersey and play too, rather than sullenly sit and watch my brother all afternoon.

There wasn't a lot of money in our house, but then there wasn't a lot of money in any of the houses of our working class community. My father switched between manual labour jobs — in forestry or the local abattoirs, or as a farmhand. Mum was a machinist, stitching shoes and leather goods. It was a simple but hard life, full of graft (work) and resourcefulness. Nothing was thrown out, and my mum went to great lengths to come up with things we needed by using the few materials she had on hand. Need a shirt for school? Your brother's from last year will do fine. Shin pads for soccer? Roll up a couple of those Reader's Digests and stuff them in your socks. Soccer shoes? These second-hand rugby boots will do the job. Goalie gloves? Hand me those mittens and I'll stitch some rubber on to the palms. There was no end to her inventiveness.

It didn't take long to figure out that items like comic books, Coke or candy were not to be expected. Such luxuries would need to be procured myself, funded by whatever means necessary — collecting pine cones for 60 cents a kilogramme, selling lemonade, cutting the neighbour's lawn. I didn't actually mind these chores. I always liked having jobs to do and projects to work on. The first sparks of my entrepreneurial spirit, perhaps.

Growing up, I was aware of our Dutch heritage — with a surname like ours, how could I not be? But there were no fireside tales about the old country, that's for sure. My father was unsentimental in that regard. Dutch was never spoken at home, so I never learnt the language. My parents later told me they did try but I recall only the most cursory of efforts — a sticky label on the TV saying 'televisie', for example. That didn't get us very far.

I suppose it was a different time and he had more pressing everyday concerns to worry about than the nature of his national and personal identity, but my father's apparent rush to shake off his Dutchness confuses me. And to be honest, it annoys me that he unilaterally made that decision for me too. I was never really given the chance to connect with our roots in a meaningful way. My father had become naturalised as a New Zealand citizen in between the births of Hans and me, which meant my brother was entitled to a Dutch passport whereas I got a New Zealand one. Don't get me wrong, I'm a proud Kiwi, but that decision ended up hurting me both ideologically and practically.

A big part of me still felt Dutch, especially at times like Christmas, when my father would bite the bullet and make the eye-wateringly expensive long-distance phone call back to Holland. The phone would be passed around a seemingly endless line of Dutch grandparents, aunts, uncles, cousins and friends. I loved hearing their accents and their tales of everyday life in Amsterdam, their promises to take me cycling along the canals when I visited. I couldn't understand why Holland only came into my life during these Christmas or birthday phone calls. My relatives were clearly desperate to remind me of and connect me to my heritage, so why did my father seem to want to close the door on that? I didn't understand it when I was young and I came to resent it as I got older.

I never did have my Dutchness formalised with a Dutch passport, which has always seemed wrong to me on an emotional level. It was a real balls up from a practical point of view too. In later years, when I wanted to study or work in Europe, I had to apply for positions as a New Zealander and painfully traipse through the visa applications. On one such occasion, when I was 20 or so, I asked my father if he was sure there was no way I could get a Dutch passport. Yes, he was a naturalised New Zealand citizen, but surely they couldn't erase the fact that he was born in Holland?

"I've already told you, Dean, I've tried calling and writing. They told me there's simply no way."

I later found out — when I was 33 — that I could have applied for the passport and been given one as a formality had I simply filled out a few forms and applied before I turned 28. I was seething when I found that out.

The passport issue is just one example of a conflict in personalities between my father and I. We didn't have a close bond when I was young and we are not that close today. His parenting style was what can only be described as old school — hard work, discipline and obedience above all. This wasn't all bad: I grew up knowing the value of a dollar, had good table manners and showed courtesy and respect to everyone, our mother above all. But things could get ugly at times, with a very 'firm heavy hand' employed for perceived infractions outside of his narrow boundaries of acceptable behaviour. I was lucky, or at least canny enough to not get on his wrong side too often, so I got off relatively lightly in comparison to my brother, Hans.

Today, my relationship with my father isn't broken — there's no animosity — but there is a cultural chasm between us. We are simply very different people. My father, like many men of his generation, is a Labour man, a socialist. Salt-of-the-earth, nothing-beats-a-hard-day's-graft type of fella. I can empathise with this view and will always appreciate his fearsome work ethic, but that is where we start to diverge.

It is as if my father used up his entire well of ambition on that first sailing from Holland to New Zealand. Today, we live in markedly different worlds with lifestyles that bear practically no relation to each other. Men of my father's generation and background are like that. They're gnarled, tough, and stubborn. Even now my father won't let me pay for a flight for him to come see me in Singapore, or for other small things. He'd sooner starve than take a free meal from someone else, least of all his youngest son. I find this attitude pretty sad, but I understand where it comes from. That's just the way it is.

So, yeah, our father-son relationship won't inspire any Hallmark cards anytime soon but I don't lie in bed crying about it.

At least I still speak to my father, which is more than I can say for my brother. Hans and I have never been close. We might have been only one year apart in age and, growing up, we spent a lot of time together. We went to the same school, played in the same sports teams and slept in the same bedroom. We shared the same surname and the same bright blond hair. In spite of all this, we couldn't be more different in personality. Hans and I rarely talked, and when we did, it was only because we were furiously arguing. Some fights got nasty and blood was spilt from time to time. I recall a garden hoe smacked into the back of my head on one occasion, a rock to the side of my face on another.

It is hard to put a finger on exactly what went wrong in our relationship, but there was jealousy at play. I was a better natural sportsman than Hans, and I did better academically too. It must have been embarrassing for him to have his kid brother run rings around him with all of his friends watching. Even when he found something he did like and was good at — cycling — I soon hopped on a bike and started clocking better times than him. This dynamic made him resentful, I think, and created the seed for a fractured relationship between us from an early age.

Things only worsened when we got into our teenage years and beyond, when his growing rap sheet for petty crime and misdemeanours contrasted pretty starkly with my lengthening list of sporting and baking achievements. A tangible distance emerged between us, and it has only grown wider over time. This isn't something I am happy about, but I have to be honest and say that, equally, it is hard to dredge up any genuine regret about it. We went in wildly different directions early in life and ended up becoming totally different people. That's all there is to it.

Baking didn't really enter my life in a significant way until my teens, a time when teachers at school started to probe about your thoughts on potential career options beyond the school walls. Good question. I had always been a determined and focused student but I didn't pull up any trees academically. I was better in the subjects that required handiwork, the likes of animal husbandry, woodwork and home economics. At 15, when it was time to select between courses to focus on for my leaving year, I chose home economics. That earned me a call to the woodwork teacher Mr Beardsley's office. He was furious that I was ditching his class in favour of home economics. As to be expected in the macho world of New Zealand, Mr Beardsley saw this as a strange decision. Home economics, after all, was for girls and "poofters". Already a stubborn so-and-so at that age, I didn't listen to a word he said. I stuck with home economics and became the only boy in the class. This suited me fine.

I can't say baking was some kind of mystical passion I was born with. Not many kids grow up dreaming of becoming a baker. I did have plenty of exposure to home baking though — every Sunday my grandmother and mum would spend hours baking scones, pies, tarts and cakes for distribution around the community or to sell at local charity fairs for a few bucks. But baking always seemed like just a domestic thing. I never thought of it as something you could make money from. It wasn't a job. In truth, when I first started doing well in home economics class, becoming a chef was the career I had in mind. It was a job I at least understood — cooks, chefs and dishwashers were at least visible in the restaurants, cafés and fast food joints around town. I rarely saw any bakers.

This impression changed dramatically, and quickly, when a man called Mr John van Til came to my high school in search of a baking apprentice. John ran an esteemed bakery in town, Rangiora Bakery, which was renowned all around New Zealand for the quality of its products. Each year John came to the school to size up the latest batch of apprentice candidates and find his latest lamb to the slaughter. His last few picks had been girls so, this time round, John rolled up knowing that he wanted a guy. Baking was heavy, hard work and he needed some height and muscle. As it turned out, he didn't have much choice. Dean Brettschneider, the only boy in class, was selected by default.

After the 'selection' had been made, John took me aside and asked, "You're not related to Jean Smith by any chance are you?"

"Actually, yes sir, I am. She's my nana, my mum's mother."

"Good, good. If you're half as hard-working and tough as Jean Smith, you won't be a complete waste of my time."

And just like that, I became an apprentice baker.

Apprenticeships might seem quaint today — maybe even unheard of for some — but back then they were highly sought after. Remember, this was a tiny rural community in New Zealand in the 1980s. Teenage kids didn't have a lot of opportunities as they looked beyond the horizons of school life. Not everyone went to college or university, as seems to be the case today, and certainly not kids like me who had a patchy-at-best academic record. Career-wise this left, well, not much — manual labour, farming, cashiers or clerks. Learning a trade, then, was a respected and valued career path.

To be clear, these apprenticeships were not a simple jaunt where you popped in a couple of times a week for a few hours, learnt a handful of techniques, baked some gingerbread men and came out a year later with a nice shiny certificate and your own little baker's hat. Apprenticeships were hard bloody work. Some might laugh, but I liken it to going to the army. You needed serious commitment and discipline to make it through.

Baking apprenticeships were run by the New Zealand Trades Certification Board, and they didn't hand out professional certification for free. Each apprenticeship lasted about five years on average, although some were completed faster, some slower — whatever it took to complete the mandated 10,000 hours of training. And once you entered this world, you were in for the long haul. Apprenticeships were not like college; there was no changing your major from sociology to psychology halfway through your degree. Decide two years into your five-year apprenticeship that this 16-hours-a-day slog of a career might not be for you after all? Tough luck, that's two years of your life lost.

Point being, you had to go into apprenticeships steeled for work and prepared to commit. This wasn't easy for many 16-year-olds. Luckily for me, I had my nana Jean Smith, whom I stayed with in Rangiora for the first eight months of my apprenticeship, to keep me right. I couldn't drive yet, so I needed to be within walking distance of the bakery. Nana Jean, the archetypal old-school rural grandmother, taught me a lot about discipline, respect and the value of an honest day's labour. She, more than anyone, was going to make sure I didn't screw up this opportunity, especially with her own good name and reputation on the line. Every morning, to the minute, I'd be woken by her banging on the door to get me up in time for the 5 a.m. shift.

Within a few weeks of hands-on work at the bakery, it became clear to me that baking was going to be my life. I still played sport and had the usual teenage distractions, but baking was number one. It helped that Rangiora Bakery had serious pedigree. In spite of its humble surroundings, this bakery was the Cambridge University, the Harvard, the Hogwarts of the baking world in New Zealand. The guys I worked with at the bakery had been working there their whole lives, some of them for more than 30 years. And they were good — very good.

It was quite a sight to see a busy bakery operating at full pelt. Everyone knew their jobs. Arms pumped like pistons kneading dough while burly bakers moved with a perverse ballet-like grace as they lifted trays in and out of the huge ovens. During intense moments, there would be no talking. These guys communicated with the merest of glances or minutest change in body language.

Trite, maybe, but I was genuinely inspired by their professionalism and quiet mastery of their craft. I was going to make sure I became that good, but I wasn't going to wait 30 years. I pestered these gnarled old veterans with questions: "How do you know when the dough is properly mixed? What do you mean by bulk fermentation? How can I slow down the staling process?" Needless to say, they found me a pain in the ass.

On first arrival, of course the shit jobs went to the rookie apprentice. Scraping trays, sweeping floors, lugging bags of flour, the usual kind of 'character-building' stuff. But after a couple of weeks — when I'd proven I wasn't a snivelling, knuckle-dragging idiot — I was expected to start contributing properly. The work was tough but rarely boring. Part of this was due to the shift rotation method instilled by John. You would do a month on pastries, a month on pies, a month on bread, and so on. Not only did this stave off suicide-inducing monotony, it exposed you to all the different types of baking early, developing your skills and expertise. It also prevented cliques forming — there were no bullshit rivalries between the cake guys and the bread guys, for example. This is one of many working practices of John's I still follow in all of my businesses today.

I threw myself into every part of the bakery I was allowed to. I wasn't satisfied with the baking side of things alone, I also tried to absorb as much as I could about the bakery as a business

— ingredients cost, shifts scheduling, delivery schedules, P&L (profit and loss) sheets. I stuck my nose into everything, sometimes to my detriment. John nearly took my head off one morning when he looked upon my trays of freshly baked vanilla slices. Ordinarily, these were bog-standard items, plain, totally unadorned. I, in my wisdom, had decided to correct this and spent a morning intricately decorating the things with delicate patterns and swirls of icing.

"Brettschneider! What the hell are these? If I ever find you wasting my icing for these poncy bollocks again, you'll be out on your arse!"

What John didn't know at that point was that we'd already sold two trays of them first thing that morning, having added 10 cents to the selling price. Those "poncy" swirls had helped move the product. Even I knew better than to raise this point in the midst of his fury with the whole staff looking on. Later that day though, when everyone else had gone home, I delicately mentioned to John that I was only trying to be proactive and help. I wasn't just pissing around; I had done my homework. I had figured out that the icing cost per vanilla slice equated to less than one cent, yet we could charge 10 cents extra from the customer. John didn't say a word, he simply nodded and sent me on my way with an eyebrow pointed to the door.

The following morning, John was already at the bakery when a co-worker and I arrived at our stations. "Brettschneider," he barked, "you're the artist. See if you can teach that reprobate mate of yours to pipe those bloody swirls on the slices. I want five trays in the shop in an hour."

That was a good early lesson in a couple of ways. It showed me that proactivity could be rewarded after all, so long as what it produced was worthwhile. It would have been easy to be cowed at the first sign of John's anger and forget the whole thing, but I stood up to him — respectfully — and ultimately won him over. But only because I had done my research and knew the numbers backed me up. If I hadn't, and it transpired that the icing cost outweighed the retail benefits? God help me.

I was prepared for a lot of graft at Rangiora Bakery, but I was surprised by the sheer extent of the physical labour involved. Lifting huge cast iron trays loaded with dense dough in and out of ovens required serious strength. On many days you didn't sit down from the first minute to the last of your shift. And you really needed to have mental discipline. Yeast waits for no man, so you had to be there on time, to the second, to put dough into the oven and take the bread out at precisely the right time. Even though I was only a teenager when I started out on the apprenticeship, I didn't resent any of this, not even the 5 a.m. starts. The discipline required for the job was part of my natural instincts and I was mature enough to rein my lifestyle in when required. I still had a good time. I went to parties and sank my fair share of beers, but I just made sure I never overdid it and was able to operate at 100 per cent during my shift the next day.

Baking was no picnic, but at least the lifestyle was friendlier than that of a chef, the occupation I might otherwise have found myself in. At least a baker has a chance at leading a somewhat functional life. A baker might work from 5 a.m. to 2 p.m., meaning an early bedtime and morning alarms in the dark, but you still have the plenty of hours left in the day to socialise, run errands and generally have a life. For a chef, it's different. They work from lunch prep right through to dinner service and beyond, maybe 11 a.m. to 10 p.m. or so, often even longer than that. And forget any time off on weekends. Such a life has led many to seek solace at their restaurant bars at the end of their killer shifts every night. It's no wonder so many of them end up as burnt-out drunks. Compared to that life, I was more than happy with my lot in baking.

Three years into the apprenticeship I was given a real break. A traditional bakery is hierarchical, like the military. At the top is the bakery owner, under him is the bakery manager, then the foreman, and after that all the rest of us plebs and nobodies. For a short time a power vacuum opened up when the bakery manager went on holiday and the foreman was suddenly sick. For a few days, chaos abounded. Seeing that nobody else was doing much to help, I stepped up to try and put things in order. I handled the inventory orders, scheduled the staff rota, mediated petty staff disputes, planned the entire week's production and everything else. I didn't do this for a pat on the back, it just needed doing and it came naturally to me. I thought nothing of it until two weeks later when I opened my pay packet and found an extra $30 in it. I told John he must have made a mistake.

"No, boy, you do the work of a foreman, you get the pay of a foreman," he said. "You'll be keeping that job too."

I'm sure I didn't totally appreciate what a big deal this was at the time, but I definitely do now. For a 19-year-old apprentice to be made foreman and given genuine leadership responsibilities over a group of staff mostly twice his age? It was a brave move by John to say the least. John clearly believed that if you're good enough, you're old enough, and this is something I agree with to this day. I think of kitchens and bakeries as the last true bastions of meritocracy. In one of my places, if I need to cut headcount and the first-year rookie is proving more dependable and baking better bread than the 20-year veteran alongside him, I'm keeping the rookie. Why wouldn't I? Experience means absolutely nothing unless it has been used to develop skills and insights that make you better at what you do. If your 'experience' simply amounts to moving from one place to the next yet learning nothing along the way, well, don't be surprised when hungrier rookies end up stealing your job.

Back in Rangiora, things were going well, and boy did I know it. That's how I ended up with the nickname FIGJAM. It wasn't because of a particularly delicious jam recipe I concocted — nah, this was an acronym for 'Fuck, I'm Good. Just Ask Me'. I took this piss-taking in my stride. I had to! I couldn't really disown the nickname. After all, I was a bit of a cocky shit, walking around like I owned the place. But I was young — 19 at the time of the promotion — so it was easy to get carried away. Anyway, in most cases the arrogance and bluster was a means of self-defence. As anyone who has worked in a busy kitchen environment knows, it is a pressure cooker atmosphere with egos and tempers flaring all the time. If you don't stand up for yourself — especially as a fresh-faced rookie — you're screwed. I gave as good as I got.

There were plenty of times in Rangiora Bakery that I upset colleagues with what I said to them, but I didn't apologise for it then and I won't now. What I said was never personal or vindictive. It was always only about professionalism. If someone didn't do what they should have done or said they would do, then they got a kick in the arse from me. Same thing today. Why should I allow my business's standards to slip because of someone else's laziness or irresponsibility? Not on my watch.

In Rangiora Bakery, many of the older guys were taken aback by a 19-year-old apprentice calling them out for cutting corners. Things often got heated. "Who the fuck do you think you are, Brettschneider? I'm twice your age, you little shit." I'd ask what that had to do with anything and remind him, firmly, that all I was doing was pointing out he had failed to carry out a job that was well understood to be his. What was the problem?

My progress as a baker and leader was marked by some early accomplishments, the most memorable two being captaining the New Zealand baking team for the Trans-Tasman Baking Trophy competition in 1987, and becoming New Zealand Baking Apprentice of the Year in 1988. These two achievements were linked in many ways, because without demonstrating serious prowess in competitions, I would never have had a shot at Apprentice of the Year.

These days, shows like the *The Great British Bake Off* have brought baking competitions into the mainstream, but the industry showdowns I was part of back in 1980s New Zealand weren't quite as glossy and glamorous as the made-for-TV productions you see today. Competitions were divided into two main categories — static displays, where you brought along your pre-made products for judging, and live 'bake-off' competitions, where you raced against the clock (and your competitors) to bake items from scratch. These two main categories were then further subdivided into 20 or more subcategories of particular products — 'Best Cupcakes', 'Best Bread', and so on.

Bakeries across New Zealand took regional and national competitions very seriously. As in any profession or trade, everyone wanted to test themselves against their peers. And it wasn't just pride being fought for. With awards came credibility, and with credibility came more customers and more cash in the till. So there was plenty to gain for Rangiora Bakery if its bakers put on a good show. In spite of this, we had to do our testing and preparation in our own time and at our own cost, outside of regular business hours.

Competitive by nature, I was made for baking contests. I also had some good fortune on my side. An English guy called Mark Shrubshall was a teacher at the college baking school where the classroom components of my apprenticeship were carried out, and Mark was the absolute t'ai chi master of baking competitions. He quickly tucked me under his wing and became another important early mentor and good friend to me. Mark came from a background of old-school patisserie baking and had spent years working in many of the grand old English hotels and country house restaurants. He had pedigree.

In the final two years of my apprenticeship, Mark and I spent a lot of time together. We were practically inseparable when a big competition was on the horizon. Every free evening and weekend I had was spent at the college with him practising. Mark taught me a lot of technical baking skills, of course, but he was most invaluable in how he prepared me for the particulars and peculiarities of baking competitions. A veteran of countless competitions himself, he had them down to a tee. The meticulousness of his preparation was on a level I had never encountered before. How to set up your table, the precise placement of your equipment (down to the centimetre and in exact order of use), how to secure a table closer to the judges — every incremental detail was sussed out. It was all about maximising efficiency and competitiveness. This 'cover all bases' approach to planning and preparation work made a big impression on me.

We were as competitive as they came at Rangiora Bakery. Christchurch was the de facto baking capital of the country because it was home to the New Zealand Baking Training Centre. This gave us somewhat of a home advantage in regional and national competitions, and we made sure we entered as many competitors in as many categories as we possibly could. During my time we were the dominant baking crew in all of New Zealand. We saw ourselves as the big dogs — unstoppable. When we arrived at a competition, a hush would descend upon the competition hall as we strutted in like rock stars. An envious sea of competitors would part for our entrance, stealing glances at our trays of perfect carrot cakes and delicate éclairs, recognising immediately that their hopes had been dashed for another year. At least, that's how I prefer to remember it.

We were good though. So much so that throughout 1987 we practically swept the board in all competitions around the country, with many of Rangiora Bakery's wins coming from the hands of yours truly. This imperious record led to the call from the New Zealand Baking Training Centre and my appointment as national captain for the Trans-Tasman showdown against Australia, to be hosted in Melbourne at the end of the 1987. That call ranks among one of my most treasured memories to this very day. It was a real shot of patriotic pride. I felt like I had been selected to go to the Olympics. But being selected was one thing, winning the damn thing was another. Mark and I simply redoubled our efforts; there was no way we were going to lose. In the end, the Aussies didn't have a chance. My team and I took the trophy home that year.

For a country boy like me, that competition in Melbourne was a big eye-opener. It was my first time in a major cosmopolitan city and everything about the experience was novel to me — a cab ride from the airport! Buildings with more than three storeys! TV screens in the hotel rooms! Competition uniforms! I walked around with my eyes popping out of my head for the whole trip. I now saw for myself what existed outside of the New Zealand bubble, a whole new world full of verve, excitement and opportunity. All of this was waiting for me, so long as I kept my head down and maintained the momentum I had built up in my fledgling baking career.

International or domestic, all the baking competitions I took part in were influential in building my confidence and making me a better baker. I usually performed well, and while the medals and prizes were gratifying, I didn't put in all that time and effort for the sake of winning a cheap plastic trophy. For me, the true reward came in the pride and satisfaction of testing my skills at the highest possible level, against my own peers, and coming out on top. After that, the test only got harder, as my competitors launched ever fiercer attempts to knock me off my perch in the next competition. But I was always there to rise to the challenge. From baking competitions to business, it's the same story today.

The Trans-Tasman success led to another. Shortly after that, I was named the New Zealand Apprentice of the Year by the New Zealand Baking Society in 1988. This was a highly competitive national title, judged by a combination of results in baking competitions, performance and conduct during your apprenticeship, and testimonials from bosses and colleagues. To think, of all the thousands of baking apprentices learning their trade all around New Zealand then, I had been named the best of the lot.

When John told me I'd won, I thought he was winding me up. I couldn't believe it. Several months prior I had even debated with him on whether it was worthwhile nominating me, as I was sure that it would be a waste of time. It was a proud achievement and an important one too; such an accolade would be a real door-opener in my career.

Honoured as I was, how the award was presented to me was a keen reminder to keep my feet on the ground. It was 1 p.m. on a typical drizzly Thursday afternoon when I heard a loud thumping and muffled shouts coming from the back door of the bakery. I apprehensively cracked open the door to be greeted by the sight of a huge guy in a stained white T-shirt looking back at me. "Where can I find Brett Schneider?"

"That would be me, Dean Brettschneider. Can I help you?"

"Ah, good. I'm Ray Walker, President of the New Zealand Baking Society. Here's your book. For Apprentice of the Year. Well done."

With that, he turned on his heel and shuffled back to his battered car. The book he had given me — my prize — was a 700-page tome called *The International Confectionaire*, a highly detailed and technical book for baking professionals with barely a single colour photograph in the whole thing. Highly useful and much treasured, yes, but not quite as glamorous as the trips to Europe or thousands of dollars of cash prizes they give the winners these days.

1988 turned out to be quite a year for me as winning Apprentice of the Year was only the start. If that hadn't been surprising and gratifying enough, another accolade came my way soon after that and nearly trumped it. The Netherlands, as I mentioned before, has a significant overseas diaspora. In a bid to promote international ties and cement connections to the homeland, the Netherlands overseas societies had a thing called Tulip Queen, sort of a pageant for young Dutch expat girls. People would nominate candidates based on their eloquence, academic and sporting records, community spiritedness — all that stuff. The winning Tulip Queen from each participating country would then get an all-expenses-paid trip to the Netherlands to take part in a competition to find the global Tulip Queen.

There was no equivalent for boys until 1988, when the inaugural Young Achiever of the Year would first be awarded. Similar to the Tulip Queen, the judges would look at school records, job performance, sporting achievements, and anything else that generally marked you as a good egg who was doing the Dutch nation proud overseas. Looking at it objectively now, I suppose I had plenty in my favour when it came to this award. I had done alright in school, I was in the first-team roster in rugby and soccer clubs, I played to a good level in tennis and cricket, and had picked up national awards in cycling. More than anything else though, there was Rangiora Bakery and my Apprentice of the Year title. Remember, this was a traditional Dutch bakery with a long and storied reputation, and John van Til was a highly respected man in Dutch society. I have no doubt an endorsement from him helped my cause. Still, when I read the letter that named me as New Zealand's Young Achiever of the Year for 1988, it was as surprising as it was thrilling.

Thankfully, unlike the Tulip Queen, there was no element of pageantry and competition for the boys. For us Young Achievers, we simply got a nice certificate and airfare for a six-week trip home to the Netherlands. It was quite a prize; given the number of flight connections involved, it must have cost a fortune. It was a marathon journey. I flew from Christchurch to Melbourne, from Melbourne to Sydney, from Sydney to Colombo, and Colombo to Abu Dhabi. At least in Abu Dhabi we had a brief break of sorts. After touchdown, the pilot came on the tannoy to inform us there would be a short stopover for refuelling. Great, I could do with a coffee and a stretch. But there would be no nice terminal or refreshments. Instead, they just dumped us outside on the tarmac under the boiling sun, affording a front seat view of the truck that came to refill the plane. 20 minutes later we were called back on board and off we went. Those were different times back then.

It was a relief, to say the least, to finally touch down at Amsterdam's Schiphol airport, after a final connection in Frankfurt. It felt like I'd been travelling for a week. I was given a hell of a welcome — as I was waiting for my bags to come round at the baggage reclaim, I glanced out at the arrivals area to see a small army of blond men and women pressed against the glass and peering eagerly through. There must have been about 15 of them. "They're keen," I thought. It wasn't until after I'd retrieved my bag and made my way closer to the arrivals hall that I realised that this was my welcome party. I had never met my extended family in person before; I only recognised them from old photographs I had seen. Dad's brother, his aunts, cousins and second cousins — even 'aunties' who weren't even related to us — were there. When I came into sight, they all started screaming in unison, "Dino, Dino! Over here!" We got some funny looks from the surrounding crowd. They must have thought we were crazy. None of us cared though, and I was so touched by the welcome. Eventually, in a blizzard of hugs, kisses, garbled chatter and a million offers to help carry my bags, we shuffled our way out and piled into a convoy of cars home.

The next six weeks were among the best of my young life. It meant a lot to be able to connect with my extended family for the first time, not to mention getting to know the country of my roots a bit. My relatives were great tour guides. We ticked off everything: the canals, the museums, the windmills and the red light district. We took a bus trip to Paris, crossed the border into Belgium, Luxembourg and Germany. It really felt like the world was my oyster. I absorbed everything I saw. Everything seemed so much more vivid and alive than in New Zealand.

Thanks to a family connection, I even took the chance to spend a week baking in a traditional Dutch bakery in a suburb just outside of Amsterdam. I learnt more about authentic European baking in that single week than I would have in a month back in New Zealand. Trust me, when I stepped back on that plane at the end of those six weeks, it was with a heavy heart, but also with the conviction that it wouldn't be long until I returned.

Back on Kiwi soil, I had the final few months of my apprenticeship to navigate in 1989. It had been quite a journey over the past four years, but as the end came within sight, I became desperate to clock the last few hours needed to complete the formalities and gain my trade certificate in baking and pastry cooking. I was hungry to join the real world and test my skills. Specifically, I was ready to test my skills overseas. I couldn't wait to get on a plane somewhere. The Trans-Tasman experience in Melbourne and those amazing six weeks in Europe the previous year were fresh in my mind, so as far as I was concerned, as soon as the ink was dry on my trade certificate, I was out of there.

I would be following a New Zealand tradition — travelling abroad at the end of your education was something many young people did. Us Kiwis call it "overseas experience", or the "Big OE". Something similar to the gap year the Brits have, I guess. However, OE wasn't just a post-school holiday, it was typically an extended trip — at least a year, often longer — with an emphasis on gathering work and life experience.

And so it was, in October 1989, armed with my freshly minted baking certificate, my CV, a folder full of testimonials and a backpack, I set off for London to begin the first major leg of my lifelong expedition in baking. It was only later that I thought of the uncanny symmetry in how my trip from New Zealand to Europe at the age of 20 was an exact reversal of the journey my father had made all those years ago when he was also 20.

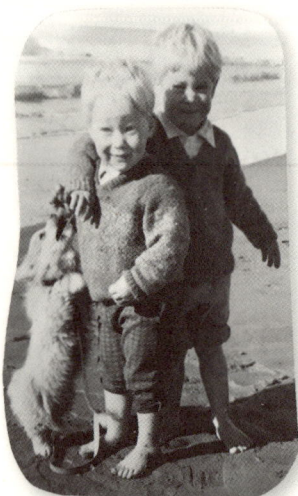

I grew up on Waikuku Beach, New Zealand with my older brother, Hans.

At a young age I was always coming up with ideas of how to make money through hard work and fun.

Dad embraced the free-spirit living of New Zealand. There wasn't a holiday we had without any time outdoors.

My Nana (Jean Smith) played a key role in my life. She even taught me how to use a butter knife in case I ever dined with the Queen one day.

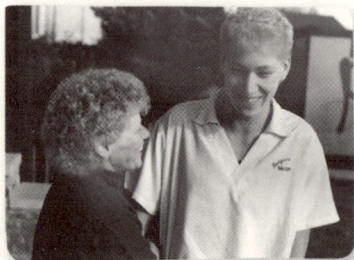

Mum and I had always been close. My focus and determination, sporting abilities and being skilled with my hands come from her.

Family portrait taken in 1985.

I played soccer (football) and was a goalkeeper at representative level. I also played rugby and tennis well, and took up cycling.

1985. I started my apprenticeship at Rangiora Bakery.

I was part of a winning team from the start. Rangiora Bakery dominated the regional and national baking competitions.

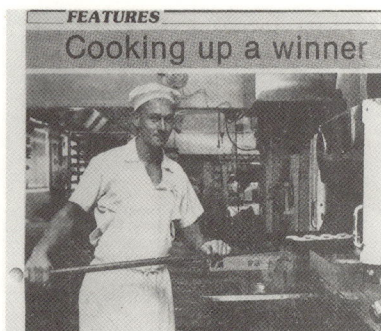

1988. Judged over the course of my apprenticeship, I was awarded the Apprentice of the Year.

I was selected to be captain of the New Zealand baking team. We competed against Australia in the Trans-Tasman Baking Trophy competition and won.

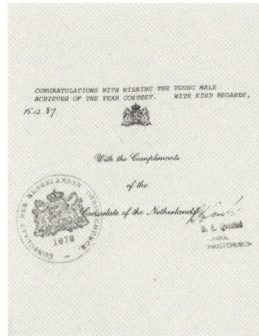

I also won the Young Achiever of the Year Award and got to travel to the Netherlands and Europe for six weeks.

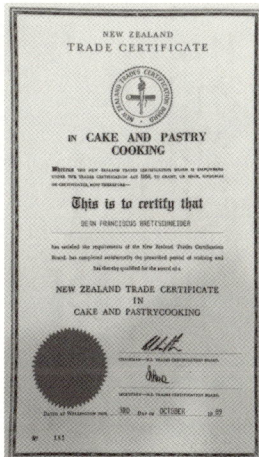

When I finally finished my baking apprenticeship, I was ready to explore the world.

Two

Mixing: Developing One's Self

After a seemingly interminable trek of flights, delays and connections, I finally reached London on a bitingly cold autumn afternoon. From Heathrow, I then wormed my way through the Underground system and eventually surfaced to drag myself to the flat of a guy called Gary Petrie, a fellow Kiwi who had agreed to let me stay with him. Gary had trodden a path in life peculiarly similar to mine. A couple of years older than me, he also hailed from Waikuku Beach. He'd gone to my high school and apprenticed at Rangiora Bakery, and now he was living overseas in search of his career dreams. Oh, and we also happened to share the same birthday. Life throws up some weird shit sometimes.

Gary was working as a pastry chef in a hotel patisserie at the time and doing okay by all accounts. His digs were modest, of course, but I was more than happy to crash on the dingy sofa in his rented flat. I was young, hungry and ready for adventure. Gary showed me the ropes and helped me find a place where I could cash my 42 (yes, really) traveller's cheques. That done, I was ready to see what the UK had to offer.

First on my to-do list was to get on a train to Manchester. This was on the back of a tip from Mark Shrubshall, my teacher and competition maestro. In my final year of apprenticeship, I was chatting with him and debating the best place for me to go for my OE. "Mate, you need to get your arse to England, and get yourself a City of Guilds qualification," he told me. Salford Technical College, located just outside of Manchester, was where Mark himself had studied, and it ran one of the country's best baking courses.

We both knew getting in to such a place would be no cakewalk. Prestigious courses like that didn't just let anyone through their hallowed doors. But I did have Mark on my side and he helped grease the wheels slightly. He put me in touch with the admissions office and got them to at least agree to look over my CV and arrange a phone interview.

Bear in mind that this was 1989 — I'm not talking about firing off a quick email with a PDF attachment and a five-minute call on Skype. In those days, cross-continental phone calls had to be booked days in advance, I even had to call the phone company to make sure our old phone was capable of calling the UK. And CVs weren't a single page document, or at least mine wasn't. My CV consisted of a 10-kilogramme cardboard box, replete with ring-bound folders of every press clipping ever written about me, copies of all of my award certificates, dozens of handwritten testimonial letters, photographs and recipes and school grades. Practically my whole life was in there. All packed up, I lugged it to the post office and paid about $100 to send it via airmail. A month after that, the admissions office finally received it and, presumably impressed by the random Kiwi on the other side of the world who was willing to go to such lengths, duly offered me an interview. I could come see them the next time I was in Manchester.

In the end, it didn't work out as I hoped. I went up there for the interview and toured the campus but, despite being accepted-in-principle, there were a couple of problems. The first was that the college intended to start me off at level one of the course. By now, I was way beyond this but the college programme wasn't in sync with the apprentice training programme in New Zealand. It was an administrative thing really, and I thought common sense could have prevailed. My ego wasn't going to let them send me back to square one; didn't they know who I was? I was reigning New Zealand Apprentice of the Year for God's sake! (FIGJAM, remember?)

The other sticking point was money. Specifically, my lack of it. Because I would be a foreign student, the college wanted £10,000 per year, which over three years, translated to about NZ$90,000 altogether. That, to put it mildly, wasn't a realistic proposition. So, yeah, there went that idea.

Plan A didn't work out, then, which left me in a bit of a dilemma, because Plan A was the only plan I had. That's the way I've always been. Even today, I don't really believe in Plan B. The way I see it, if you have a Plan B already in mind, then you don't have enough faith in Plan A. You're set up to fail before you begin. I reckon if you prepare assiduously and work hard enough, Plan A should work in all but the most extreme of cases.

I took this setback in stride. It wasn't the end of the world. It also helped that, before sending me on my way, a staff member at Salford Technical College enquired about my next move during my stay in the UK. If I wouldn't be joining their course, would I be interested in a baking job he knew of in Croyden, London?

Sounded good to me, and that's how I ended up working in an in-store bakery of a Sainsbury's supermarket. Fair enough, not the most glamorous of gigs, but whose first job is? I saw it as a chance to gain some hands-on experience and get to know how big in-store retail baking worked.

Sainsbury's might be seen as a decaying and stale chain today, but when I was there in 1989, it was a market leader and far more dynamic in everything it did. Its in-store bakeries were top notch. Every single item sold in the baked goods section was made fresh in-house daily. This is very different from the norm today, where almost everything is brought in from third-party purveyors. I wasn't there for long — just a couple of months — but I learnt a lot about system-based working; the importance of judicious stocktaking; and how to deal, cajole and banter with a wide network of workmates, suppliers, bosses and customers. It was another useful step on my learning journey.

(It also helped that the bakery manager — an absolute beauty from Manchester — took a shine to me. Suffice to say we found ways to pass the time during the slower periods.)

Working in Sainsbury's for two months was alright, but I knew I had more to learn. I chatted a lot with Gary about his experiences in London's red-hot fine dining scene and I quite liked the idea of trying my hand as a pastry chef. This would be a different world compared to what I had been doing up to that point. In Rangiora I was in a traditional bakery, producing all the products associated with that. A pastry chef still bakes, of course, but is based in a professional kitchen in restaurants and hotels, preparing desserts and other baked goods to order for diners. In the London dining scene of that era, patisserie baking meant old-school European desserts — very technical, difficult little bastards. Moving to a professional kitchen environment was a calculated move. To keep developing, I knew I needed to keep adding strings to my bow.

I walked to the nearest recruitment agency and told them all this. The recruiter liked the Apprentice of the Year award and numerous other achievements emblazoned all over my CV, but to be a pastry chef you needed experience in restaurants or hotel kitchens. Did I have any? Some bullshitting later — a skiing holiday I'd had in Canada suddenly turned into a three-month stint at one of North America's finest hotels — and I had a job at the Royal Festival Hall on Southbank.

I'd been sleeping on Gary's couch for a few months by now, and with a job secured, I figured I could take a small step up the rental ladder. To do so, I cashed in on a tenuous connection. A mate of mine from New Zealand had a cousin who worked as a banker for Goldman Sachs in the city. He was called Stuart. I had only ever met Stuart once years ago at a party back home. He told me then — after his sixth or seventh beer — that I should look him up if I ever found myself in London. It was just one of those throwaway comments people make and never think twice about again. Imagine the poor guy's face, then, when two years later he picks up the phone to hear, "Stuart! It's me, Dean, your cousin's mate. I made it to London after all. What's your address?" Fair play to him though — he stuck to his word.

Things were taking shape. Now with a rented room and a job, I settled into a routine. Stuart's flat was in Erith, a suburb an hour from the City of London by train, so I had to be up before sunrise to catch the first train of the day. After working my way through the Underground to Waterloo East station, I'd surface and enjoy a precious few minutes of fresh air during the walk to the Royal Festival Hall at Southbank before taking my post in the dungeon kitchens deep in the bowels of the building.

The Royal Festival Hall, as the name suggests, hosted music and art performances, conferences and talks, and was home to many restaurants and cafés. Naturally, the F&B demands in such a place were huge. I quickly understood why the recruiter had placed such a big emphasis on experience. Talk about being thrown in to the deep end. Initially, I got my ass kicked in that kitchen. The restaurant world was frantic, non-stop. The pressure was so much more intense than it had been in the bakery. In a bakery, you worked hard, but as long as you knew your stuff and had your shit in order, you were fine. This was different. Now there might be a banquet room upstairs filled by 1,000 people (VIPs, of course — everyone seemed to be a bloody VIP in that place) currently schmoozing their way through their entrées. That meant in 15 minutes, a thousand tart citrons with raspberry coulis had to be ready to go from the pastry section, all at the same time.

This was a valuable crash course on the fundamentals of pastry cooking. Every day I was making crème brûlée, panna cotta, macarons — sophisticated European desserts that were a world away from the hot cross buns and loaves of bread I was cranking out in Rangiora. Sure, I'd done these types of desserts before, and I knew the theory from my studies, but not like this. This was the real deal, on the front line. It wasn't just learning patisserie techniques, it was learning to execute them under high pressure, which is a totally different skill altogether. On top of this, I began seeing the importance of presentation, placing and symmetry, appreciating the whole theatre of a beautifully constructed dessert.

Those first few months as a pastry chef in London were intoxicating. Moving from a small town New Zealand bakery to this was like black and white television going full colour. I was part of huge cosmopolitan baking teams — French, Italians, Nigerians and Peruvians, you name it. I learnt a lot from this melting pot of cultures, mostly different swear words in 15 different languages. In any kitchen, teamwork was crucial. This meant the camaraderie was great when things were going well, but you were never far from a serious dressing down if you fucked something up and let the whole team down.

The hours were crazy. I'd find myself in the kitchen from 6 a.m. until 2 p.m., where I'd be sent on my way with a warning to be back at 5 p.m. for the dinner shift. That was no use to any of us — London was a big place and we didn't have the time nor money to go home and come back again. Because of this, many afternoons were spent napping on park benches. After dinner service, we might get out at 10 p.m. — time for one pint before the last train home, we'd say. Eight drinks later and three hours after the last train had left the station, we'd stagger over to the hotel we worked at. There we'd drunkenly bribe the security guard and flirt with the cute girl at reception, hoping to be shown enough pity to be sneaked into a free guest room for a couple of hours kip (rest).

For a young man experiencing the real world for the first time, it was a thrilling life. But it was exhausting. I kept up with the work hard, party hard routine for approaching a year — jumping around a couple of different jobs in the restaurant business — but the 18-hour work days were becoming a real strain. Plus, as cutting edge and glamorous as the fine dining scene might have been — this world of Marco Pierre White,

Albert Roux and La Gavroche — the pay was a joke. Excepting the head chef (who was never around anyway), everyone got paid shit, and for those of us at the bottom of the food chain, we were paid the shittiest. Customers might have been paying £100 per head for a meal at the restaurants I worked at, but there was no trickle-down economics in the food industry. I made £3.75 per hour at the best of times, not even enough for an appetiser at the very restaurant I was working for.

That summer, I got off the treadmill for a couple of months to gift myself a late 21st birthday present of a backpacking trip around Europe. With that break, on which I hitch-hiked around Denmark, Sweden, Germany and Holland, I bookended an electrifying first year of my OE with travelling. It had been a rollicking time of grafting, partying, dodging and learning. I had relished every minute and was thirsty for more — right after my holiday.

I came back from my backpacking sojourn refreshed and ready for my next move. There was a job waiting for me. A couple of months prior, I was flipping through the job ads in an industry magazine and one particular job jumped off the page at me. It was a role to set up a bakery from scratch, in a grand old country hotel in a place called Beaulieu, a picturesque village on the edge of the New Forest National Park in Hampshire. After a successful interview with the head chef, I was offered the job and told to come back in a few months when the the basic construction work on the bakery was finished. That time had now arrived, so I bagged up my few possessions, found someone to take over my room rental in London and in the late autumn of 1990, hopped on a train to my new rural outpost.

Beaulieu represented quite a change from London. This place was the quintessential English rural village. Cobblestone streets, red letterboxes, rolling green fields and pretty little streams — the full Downton Abbey experience. The Montagu Arms Hotel, of which the new bakery would be part of, fitted into this picture perfectly. It had a lovely red brick facade, on which green ivy grew pleasingly up the walls and flower baskets hung in front of charming cross-hatch windows. It was the kind of place you imagined tweed-wearing gentlemen retiring to for a fortifying glass of sherry and a cigar after a successful day's hunting. Actually, that was the kind of place it was.

The Montagu Arms wasn't just another run-of-the-mill pretty hotel. It was owned by a corporate powerhouse in the food and hospitality scene that didn't mess around. The hotel's restaurant, The Terrace, was one of the most revered fine dining places in the south of England and boasted a coveted Michelin star. The place had prestige. This reputation was an attraction for me, but the main factor that persuaded me to leave the London scene was the chance to be a key figure in building a brand new bakery from the ground up. It was a rare and exciting opportunity.

The owner wanted a classic French boulangerie concept — honest, simple, delicious breads, pastries and desserts. The products would serve three outputs: over-the-counter retail at the bakery itself, the hotel's restaurant needs, and wholesale supply to some surrounding businesses. Of course, the owner knew his numbers, but he knew nothing about baking. He told me he wanted a young and innovative team to take up the challenge. That was where I came in, together with the guy who was going to run the place, a Frenchman by the name of Richard Bertinet.

Richard was a native of Brittany, where he had done his bakery training, and he was there to put the French in our French boulangerie concept. That's not to say he was a mere mascot. Richard could only have been in his mid-to-late twenties at that stage, but he had already built an impressive résumé and was well known in the fine dining scene of rural England after a string of stints at noted restaurants with big name chefs. One of his best mates was the future celebrity chef Jean-Christophe Novelli, who was then cooking at a successful restaurant not too far away in Lymington Spa. (Later, after we had both left the Montagu, Richard played a role in Novelli's surge to stardom, acting as his operations manager for his London enterprises.)

I liked Richard from the first time I met him. I still do. He was a charismatic and gregarious character, a hard worker who's passionate about baking, but also the type who knew how to blow off some steam too. A guy after my own heart. We both threw ourselves into equipping the bakery and getting it ready for opening. Our new bakery had previously been a humble staff canteen, so size-wise, it was compact. The blueprints were well designed and efficient though, so we had enough space — just — for our benches, mixers, ovens and trolleys. It would be a squeeze, but it would do us just fine.

Business was nuts from day one. We all knew it would be busy, but few of us were prepared for just how mad it turned out to be. Richard and I were always the first to arrive, usually around 3 a.m., to start baking everything we needed for our three-pronged output. There was no let up. As soon as the over-the-counter stuff was safely in the oven, it was then time to start working on the restaurant service — breakfast, lunch and dinner. Around that, we had to think about the extra wholesale product. It was staggering how much we created from that confined little space.

Our product was good — very good. It was at the Montagu where I truly learnt the craft of baking. My training and experiences thus far had made me an adept baker in some ways — I could crank out delicious bread and buns in my sleep — but I had not yet had much exposure to the sophistication of French-style baking. Culturally, the type of baking done in New Zealand was a world away from what French boulangeries were doing. In Rangiora Bakery, the old-timers referred dismissively to baguettes as "French sticks", which were then made by taking basic white bread dough and rolling it long. Under Richard's tutelage I quickly came to appreciate the true art and craft behind the fabled baguette and its other baked relatives.

The philosophy was simple: a true artisan baker should work with only natural ingredients, particularly the fundamental four of water, yeast, flour and salt. Most bakers rely on a wide plethora of artificial additives and improvers to enhance their products in a variety of ways, such as shelf life, texture and taste. Such improvers and additives, however, were a big no-no in a French boulangerie.

Stripping down baking to only its most essential ingredients makes baking much more of a challenge. Without the crutch of artificial additives providing shortcuts and escape routes, a baker really needs to know his shit, to really understand the science of baking. Time, temperature and fermentation all now become utterly crucial. A simple, minor miscalculation and your whole batch is screwed. But get it right and what comes from the oven is the most fragrant, delicious and authentic product that man can make.

Richard and I made a good team. He was undoubtedly the brain behind our best artisan breads, but I would piss myself watching his attempts to decorate a cake. Or when he tried to do anything except bread, in fact. But that's what I was there for, after all, and I held my end up well enough. Jean-Christophe Novelli himself came by one evening for dinner and after trying one of my chocolate logs, he told me it was one of the best he'd ever tasted. Soon after, Novelli was ordering batches from us to sell as a dessert at his own Michelin-starred restaurant.

Today, Richard would likely admit his patisserie skills were not the best back in those days, but he wasn't so forthcoming with the truth at the time. Richard was the charming, cultured French baker, and all our customers naturally assumed the delicate soufflés, éclairs and tarts had come from his magisterial hands. Richard was in no rush to tell anyone that the true artist was the rugged Kiwi guy who came to work in shorts every day.

This is why I relished the times wealthy wives would blag (con) their way into the kitchen to implore the handsome Frenchman to personally decorate a cake for their upcoming teenage daughter's birthday party. I'd let Richard sweat it out for a few minutes, spewing icing unevenly all over the cake like a Jackson Pollock painting, his soon-to-be-former admirers looking on with gazes ranging from bemusement to horror. After he'd suffered enough, I'd come to his rescue, calling him to an imagined emergency outside before salvaging the cakes myself. I earned countless post-work drinks from Richard this way.

An interesting aspect of life at the Montagu was how many of the hotel staff lived on-site, in what was called the staff cottage, which was a short walk from the hotel itself. There were 15 or so of us in there — the maître'd, the sommelier, the receptionist, some of the waitresses — and all of us were similarly young and free. This created a real collegiate atmosphere and we had a lot of fun. At the end of every service, all the staff retired to the staff cottage for an after-hours party. Any hotel guests we could pick up on the way were more than welcome to join us. These parties weren't quite the Last Days of Sodom, but we definitely lived up to the work hard, play hard maxim.

A regular attendee at these parties was a very pretty, demure young woman called Susan Edyvean, the hotel receptionist. Hailing from Cornwall, Susan was the very definition of 'a good girl'. Effortlessly polite, heart of gold, a little awkward and shy. The type of girl mums and grandmothers fawn over. I took a liking to Susan straight away. And for her part, she seemed taken by the boisterous baker from New Zealand who strutted around the place like he owned it.

Susan, being both beautiful and friendly, was a popular target of many a young member of Montagu staff, past and present. I had been warned that there was no point wasting my time on the earnest good girl on reception, whom they had come to call "Susan Ever-virgin". It was unwitty and infantile, and Susan just laughed the nickname off, often firing back with far more barbed ripostes of her own. In any case, not long after I had set my eyes on her — and much to the disbelief of our colleagues — Susan and I became an item. That stupid nickname could be retired for good.

We stayed together even after Susan left the hotel some months later to take up a new job working on cruise ships. A long-distance relationship wasn't fun, but we made the best of it. We were both working so hard anyway that it took our minds off each other's absence. We kept in touch through letters and long-distance calls, which, in those days were dialled from huge, box-shaped, wall-mounted phones. We had one in the Montagu staff quarters but, fuck me, overseas calls were expensive. I had already learnt my lesson after the boss deducted $100 from my pay for a 10-minute call to my parents during my first week in the hotel. I liked Susan, but not at that rate.

So, summoning my Kiwi handyman spirit, I followed the phone's cables to a plastic circuit box at the bottom of the wall. I removed the plastic casing from that and figured out a way to rig the handset of a second phone into the circuit board and bypass the modem. Hey presto, free overseas calls. Well, I say free, but I mean free for me. A former colleague later told me that the phone company eventually found out what was going on and sent the hotel a monumental bill shortly after I left. Hopefully they've gotten over the shock by now.

My time at the Montagu was when I truly first came to appreciate how baking belonged in the real food world. A world of restaurants, menus, chefs, waiters, cafés. This might seem stupidly obvious, but remember that the 1990s looked very different to 2019. The café culture explosion hadn't happened yet. In those days, for many people, baking meant bread — and bread was just bread. Your morning slice of toast, a stale roll that accompanies a bowl of soup, a bland-tasting sandwich from the convenience store. When people thought of cakes or hot-cross buns, that brought to mind a trip to the town bakery, a specialised place where you went to pick up your baked item to take away in a box and eat at home. Baking had an association with a domestic or home environment, not an external dining one.

What I'm saying is that cooked food and baked food were regarded as wildly different things. They co-existed, sure — a steak and a gateau will both still appear on the same menu — but it was an unequal relationship, with baked goods often seen as the frivolous, lesser partner to the more serious cooked stuff. Chefs got more respect than bakers and the entrée was the unquestionable star section of the menu. It's just the way it was.

But not at the Montagu. There I learnt that real baking went much beyond the idea of a bakery. Much of our time and effort were directed towards our Michelin-starred restaurant. Urgent orders were frequently barked to us from the kitchen from morning to night. The head chef needed our stuff "right now!" He needed it, not as a dull adornment to his meal, but as a crucial partner to the whole dish.

Would the chef's steamed mussels have the same impact without the crusty, freshly baked garlic bread that went with it? Where would his duck pâté be without the still-warm, butter-infused baguette? In other dishes, baking and cooking were literally intertwined. Richard, the head chef and I might spend hours together perfecting a beef Wellington recipe, testing and retesting until the crispy pastry coat complemented the meat enclosed within just the way we wanted. Sometimes, baking even had the chance to take centre stage by itself — ever had a good doughless pizza?

Richard and I were lucky in that our restaurant's head chef understood food — really understood it. Good chefs appreciate how crucial baking is. Shit chefs generally don't, which is why their careers and restaurants tend to never get far. Our chef — also like all good chefs — was a control freak. "That brioche you're making is 1 cm too wide for my plates," he told us one day. "Give me stuff that actually fits on my fucking plates." From then on, that meant an extra hour each day baking a special batch just for him.

Another time, our chef went to a trade show in Paris and came back raving about the caramel cages he saw some of the Europeans doing. We didn't have a clue what he was talking about. Luckily, I found the recipe in an old reference book and a week later we had our very own caramel cages to boast about, the only ones in our part of England at the time. Richard and I loved this innovative, creative dynamic between the bakery and the kitchen. Just the way it should be.

I mentioned earlier Jean-Christophe Novelli singling out my chocolate log for praise, and there were other moments like it. The head chef of Park Lane Hotel in London passed through one day and, after his meal, he asked to see Richard and me personally to compliment us on the desserts his group had just enjoyed. He left his card and told us to call in for dinner the next time we were in London. When we took him up on his offer a few months later, the chef came out to greet us at our table, again commending us on the quality of our work.

Seeing the true importance of baking in the wider food world was my Paul on the road to Damascus moment. The scales had fallen from my eyes. Before then, I always had pride in my work, but now I had even greater belief in what I was doing and more self-respect because of that. As a paid-up member of the Real Food World, I now saw that the doors of the entire F&B industry were open to me.

Discovering this perspective so early in my career was crucially important as it meant I went forward with my horizons wide open from the beginning. I was a baker, yes, but I could also be a cook, an entrepreneur, a businessman, a teacher, a writer… If I had instead spent the first five years of my career doing nothing but bake bread and buns in a provincial bakery, then who knows when this realisation would have hit me, or whether it would have at all?

As great as my Montagu experience was, towards the end of 1991 I handed in my resignation and started packing my bags for home. Two immediate factors made it seem like the time was right. My mate Johnny had asked me to be his best man at his wedding back in New Zealand, and I was determined to be back for that. My two-year work visa was by now coming to an end too. The clock on that had started ticking the first day I arrived in London.

On top of that, after almost a year at the Montagu, I had started to tire of the rural English countryside. The work was rewarding, sure, but outside of that there wasn't a lot for a 22-year-old to do. I also have to admit that, as gung-ho and independent as I was, I was still only a young guy and I'd now been away from home for two years — I missed my friends and family. Yeah, the time was right to go home.

1998. I was the first in my immediate family to visit my father's birth home in Amsterdam ever since he left all those years ago.

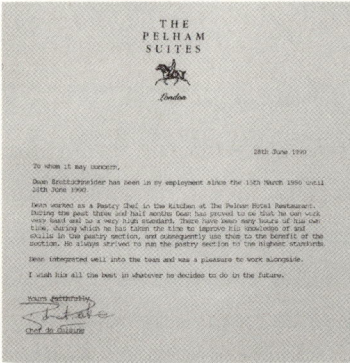

London was where I honed my skills as a pastry chef.

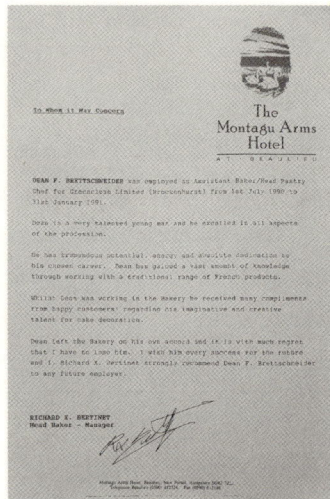

At 21, I worked with Richard Bertinet at The Montagu Arms Hotel. 30 years later, I've made a name for myself, and so has he — although on different sides of the world.

I worked as a pastry chef at The Montagu Arms Hotel along with
fellow baking extraordinaire Richard Bertinet.

Three

Maturing: The Student Becomes The Teacher

I suppose the clichéd, lofty goal of any OE is to gain useful work experience and come back a better person. Trite as it sounds, that rings true for me. I had left New Zealand with all the credentials and certificates a young baker could hope for, but little by way of real-life experience, and nothing beyond the shores of New Zealand. My two years away had changed that. Now I had hands-on work experience ranging from baking bread for a chain supermarket, to perfecting soufflés en masse in an international conference venue, and setting up a successful new artisan bakery in a countryside hotel. The way I saw it, I had been thrown in the deep end and, far from sinking, I had swum the fucking butterfly stroke.

My efforts were appreciated by all the bosses I had worked for my and the peers I had worked with in England. I returned home with an armload of references from some serious names in the food business. In those pre-internet days, these old-fashioned, hard-copy references did not come easy. They were worth more than their weight in gold, especially in New Zealand, where not many bakers could compete with the kind of endorsements I had compiled.

With my bolstered new CV in hand, it didn't take long to find a job on my return home. I was offered a position as test baker for Ernest Adams, a 60-year-old industrial bakery that produced ready-made traditional cakes, breads and cookies. They were a hugely successful homegrown company. A household name and very traditional, Ernest Adams was the McVities of New Zealand. I was stationed in their head office in Christchurch, complete with my crisp new uniform: a white laboratory coat and a pair of goggles.

Industrial baking on this scale was totally new to me. The products we made were very familiar — pound cakes, sultana cakes and slices, all the quintessential English stuff — but here we were baking enough to feed an entire country, not just a few dozen customers from the village. When you are making stuff in that kind of quantity, the entire science of baking changes. You needed to think about how different ingredients, their combinations and the baking processes involved affected a staggering number of variables, most important being the total possible yield and the shelf life. The trick was to figure out ways to create products in huge quantity that lasted for ages and tasted good enough for people to want to eat them.

Of course, the company's real boffins, genuine food scientists and mathematicians, did the complicated calculations. They had brought me in to focus on creativity, innovation and taste. Although Ernest Adams could pump out a billion criss-cross buns that could last on the shelf for two years if they wanted, they needed people like me to find ways to make them look and taste good. And, importantly, to find ways to make them look and taste just different enough to relaunch them as a new line the following year.

As can be deduced from the term 'test baker', trial and error was often the only way to find out if one thing worked better than another. Take sultanas for example: no two types are the same and each type has its own particular properties that respond differently in the baking process. So to find out which works best in a particular recipe, we would bake God knows how many batches of bread, with each batch using different brands of sultanas. But that was just the start. With the different breads now baked, how do we define 'best'? Is it Sultana A, the best tasting one? Or Sultana B, the one that lasts longest? Then what about Sultana C, which is not too bad on either score, but happens to be the cheapest by far? Every product presented its own basket of conundrums like this. Finding ways to solve these riddles made the job challenging and rewarding — and sometimes made you want to put your fist through the wall.

From what I'd been doing in the Montagu Arms with Richard mere months before, this was a world apart. From lovingly hand-crafting bespoke brioche (to the centimetre), now I was working in a lab coat, looking upon industrial ovens bigger than the Montagu's entire bakery. But it was different, something new to learn about, which was precisely why I was there. Like all of my earlier career moves, this was a strategic choice to procure more skills and knowledge. I didn't want to be the best at merely one aspect of baking; I wanted to be great at everything.

Come the new year in 1992, I had a notable new colleague at Ernest Adams — Susan. We had somehow kept things together long distance since she had left to work on the cruise ships. As soon as she had learnt I was moving back to New Zealand, she earnestly told me over the phone that she'd join me as soon as she got back to shore. There was some vacillation, which was to be expected, but after some hand-wringing, she flew out to join me after the Christmas holidays.

It can't have been an easy decision for Susan to leave her family and friends to go and throw her lot in with a guy on the other side of the world, especially considering our relationship amounted to little more than a few-months-long fling and a handful of long-distance calls. There were times I was sure she wouldn't be able to do it, but fair play to her, she was brave. I was — I am — very glad she made the decision she did.

There commenced a pretty quiet period of life for us. Susan got a job in the accounts department of Ernest Adams and we moved in together. We stayed in the spare room of my parents' house for a few months initially before we got our own place in Christchurch. Susan made some friends in the community and I got involved with the rugby club again. Using the company car I'd been given, we took drives to the surrounding countryside together. It was very pleasant and sedate, but we weren't complaining. After the hectic lives we'd spent in bakeries and boats for the past few years, we were glad to have the downtime.

That's not to say I was ready to embrace early-onset middle age. I kept on my toes and, with the help of some old friends, found new avenues of interest outside of the day job. The first enterprise involved a baker by the name of John Kjuipers, another mentor figure for me. We had been mates for years and our paths had often crossed over the years in the local baking world. John ran a successful bakery in Christchurch and he was to prove instrumental in my first entrepreneurial breakthrough.

It all started with an influential trip to the US I had been on in 1991. I was sent by Ernest Adams to attend a course at the American Institute of Baking (AIB) as part of my product development and technical responsibilities. Without going into too much detail, the course revolved around the most recent research and development of frozen dough. Sometimes referred to as 'bake-off' items, or parbaking, this was, essentially, frozen ready-to-bake dough that companies like mine developed and sold to supermarkets, negating the need for machines and mixes — they just needed to pop these frozen doughs in the oven and proof them off. These kinds of products were big business in the US at the time, but practically unheard of in New Zealand.

That course was an enlightening insight for me into the science of baking and the potential technology had to shape and change our industry, something I have never forgotten. I was practically shaking with excitement on the flight home after that trip, ready to tell everyone at Ernest Adams how we were going to create and build our own portfolio of frozen dough products and corner the domestic market. Which we promptly did. That was a nice feather in the cap for a young and ambitious executive.

But it wasn't just frozen dough I learnt about on that American trip. I was also inspired by a demonstration by one ingredients company that talked about different items that were most suitable for large-scale industrial production. One product really jumped out at me: butter flake rolls. These were light, fluffy, flaky dinner rolls that I couldn't recall ever seeing in New Zealand. They were delicious. I was certain they would be a massive hit for Ernest Adams. I duly reported back but, for whatever reason, they disagreed with me and passed on the idea.

Venting, I told John this during a visit to his bakery one evening. His interest quickly piqued, John asked me if I knew the recipe. We ended up baking a batch on the spot and from his very first taste, John knew we were on to something. His bakery wasn't huge in retail terms but he sold a lot of wholesale products to shops, restaurants and other small businesses. We decided to roll these out in his bakery as a test and see how they went.

Fuck me, did they sell. John couldn't keep up with the demand. Within a week he was selling 3,000 of these bloody things a day. There started a frantic few weeks of trying — and failing — to bake the rolls faster than people were buying them. Every night after work I went straight to his bakery and, with Susan's help, the three of us kneaded, rolled and baked through the night, rushing against the clock to be ready for the delivery vans coming to pick them up at 3 a.m. We thought this was our ticket to becoming millionaires. We were getting a royalty of $0.10 per roll sold, after all.

Some months into this back-breaking routine, it became clear that this was not sustainable. None of us were getting any sleep, and while the extra pocket money was good, it wasn't worth the hassle. So, having learnt about intellectual property, franchising, licensing and the like from my work at Ernest Adams, I drew up my first ever franchise manual for the butter flake rolls. The manual contained the recipe, the ingredients, step-by-step sketches, costings — everything. I went to the local print shop and had it nicely laminated, then drove to John's and sold it to him for $2,000. He carried on using the recipe for years afterwards and, by all accounts, did well out of those rolls. A win-win for all.

My first ever franchise deal. $2,000 wasn't life-changing, but it was a real buzz to have made money directly from my own creativity and sense of entrepreneurship. To sell a loaf of bread, a tangible product, is one thing, but to sell a concept, an idea —

that was an exhilarating feeling. So this is what business is. It was an eye-opening moment.

That first successful franchising deal in 1991 — micro-scale as it was back then — demonstrated how I was quickly developing a business acumen, for which I have to give Ernest Adams a lot of credit. They had sent me on a battery of courses to sharpen things like presentation skills, report writing, effective networking, all that sort of stuff. I really got stuck into all of it, and the results spoke for themselves. Soon, I was comfortable flying to international trade shows and pitching (successfully) to senior executives at some of the world's biggest supermarket brands. I was beginning to get a firm grasp on the business world of baking, which set me in good stead for the rest of my career. I consider that little deal with John for those butter flake rolls as my first true business milestone.

Another important figure to reappear at around this time was my old mucker Mark Shrubshall. He asked me if I'd like to teach part-time night classes at the New Zealand Baking Training Centre in Christchurch Polytechnic, where he was still working. The job at Ernest Adams was a nine-to-five gig, so I had plenty of free time to kill. I happily took Mark up on his offer.

Initially, I did two night classes a week at the college. My bosses at Ernest Adams didn't mind — in fact they encouraged it. It didn't affect my work for them and it also kept my creative juices flowing, so no problems there. Straight off the bat, I took to teaching like a duck to water. I surprised myself by how much I enjoyed it and how much the students seemed to as well. After all those years as apprentice and student, I was now in the role of teacher and mentor.

It helped that these weren't lifestyle or hobby classes but serious lessons where young people's lives and future careers were on the line. It was a privilege, really, to be entrusted with such responsibility in young people's lives. I hoped I could prove as influential to my students as Mark had been for me several years earlier. For Ernest Adams's part, they too recognised my passion for teaching and asked me to mentor the apprentices they had working with us, so, suddenly, it seemed like every spare moment I had was spent nurturing young bakers.

I quickly developed an affinity for teaching. It felt natural and I relished seeing the impact I was having on the students. It was a logical decision, then, to say yes when the New Zealand Baking Training Centre offered me a full-time position. I was midway through my second year at Ernest Adams by that point, and while I was very appreciative of the faith they had shown in me, I was starting to get itchy feet from the everyday routine. Working nine to five was never really me. Still, I learnt a lot in that time and I retain a lot of respect for that company. Even when I sheepishly handed in my resignation, my boss handled it with a lot of understanding and sent me on my way with best wishes. That was good of him. It would have been understandable for him to give me a boot in the ass instead.

I was 23 at this stage, unusually young to be a full-time baking teacher, but I'd already packed a lot into a seven-year career: Apprentice of the Year, many diverse jobs in respectable and not-so-respectable establishments, various prizes and competition wins. Even though most of the students were only a couple of years younger than me, I had pedigree and they respected that.

Still, I knew that the length of my CV and stack of fancy credentials would only get me so far with these 19-year-olds, and some of them didn't give a shit anyway. To gain their trust and create my authority, I would have to prove my skills. That was no problem. They quickly saw that I could bake a fucking good loaf of bread. And beyond the technical side of things, I had by now become a more patient character. I was able to connect with the students on a personal level and encourage them. The FIGJAM years — luckily for them — were largely behind me by that point.

On a serious note, this was an important aspect of my personal development. Had I come to teaching a few years earlier, I'm not sure I would have been very good for it. I really didn't have much time for people who couldn't keep up or didn't seem to be on the same wavelength as me. It wasn't that I didn't know what empathy was — of course I did — but perhaps I didn't apply it as much as I should have. But now, I found I was able to put myself in the students' shoes to understand how and why they were finding a particular concept or technique difficult to master. Once I had cracked that, it was then a simple task of adjusting my method of instruction or explaining it in a different way to help them grasp the point. There was always a surge of satisfaction every time those breakthroughs came.

That's not to say I ran an easy ship. I ran my classrooms like a sergeant major. If classes started at 8.30 a.m., then the door was locked at 8.30 a.m. Show up at 8.31 a.m. and you can piss off. You've just wasted your entire day of class as you're not getting in. If I sensed any disrespect or inattention while I was teaching, well, God help you. My classes were tight and disciplined, but they were fair, built on the principle of mutual respect. For those who were committed to working as hard as I did, I was there for them, for whatever they needed and as long as it took. But the slackers and jokers could go and jump off a bridge for all I cared.

My methods bore fruit. It wasn't long into my full-time role that it was time to start preparing the New Zealand team for the annual Trans-Tasman Baking Trophy competition in Australia, the very same competition in which I captained New Zealand to victory six years earlier, the starting point that led to Apprentice of the Year and all the experiences that had followed it. Just like six years ago, the New Zealand team returned from Melbourne with winner's medals around their necks, leaving the trounced Aussies in their wake. Sometimes history does repeat itself.

For the first year of teaching full-time, I loved it. I really did. It was a new experience, a new environment, and I was learning as much as the students were. But then — and I remember this feeling coming on quite suddenly — I started to find it becoming stale. I returned from school one Friday evening feeling fine about things but come the following Monday morning, an uncanny sense of malaise settled over me on the drive to work.

Course-teaching, by nature, is structured and repetitive. A syllabus is set for each batch of apprentices and you work through the textbook, page by page, until the end of the year. Hopefully enough stays in the kids' heads and they don't balls up the exams. The next year, a fresh batch of apprentices shuffles into the classroom, ready to begin their course. "Okay, turn to page one of your manual." Rinse and repeat. Now in my second year of teaching, I was cycling through the same stuff. This was only a few years after undergoing the exact same course as a student myself. If I wanted to, I could have practically recited the manual from memory, word for word, copyright page included.

Fuck me, I thought in the car that Monday morning, I'm bored of this. I didn't hate the job — far from it —but if I was already feeling this way after only 14 months of it, clearly it was time to move on. Teaching would be a better fit later in life when I was winding down, but not right now when I was just getting started.

That 14-month window of teaching was invaluable to me, though. Organisation, planning, demonstration: these were three fundamentals that were demanded of you if you were to have even half a chance of surviving as a baking teacher. Easily distracted teenagers suffered no fools gladly, so you had to have your shit together. To lose focus for even 10 minutes in front of them could all too easily create distraction and, while no class of mine ever descended into anarchy, restless students and a disorganised environment is a dangerous combination that quickly destroys lessons.

My lesson plans, then, were planned with a level of detail that some might describe as excessive. To that I say there is no such thing as excessive detail. Every minute, literally, was planned out. And it was the same prep-wise. My equipment, my ingredients, my reference materials — all selected, portioned and positioned in the order I needed them and in such a way to ensure I didn't so much have to stretch to reach what I needed. This let me work fast and demonstrate techniques to the class clearly.

I credit those early years spent as a teacher for really hammering home those fundamentals in myself. So much of what I've done since has been built on that foundation of comprehensive organisation and meticulous planning, whether it's training staff, doing corporate demonstrations, writing books, appearing on TV or working at my baking school. It seems so simple in theory, and in truth it should be, but I am frequently shocked by how many professionals of different walks of life fail to take proper preparation seriously enough.

As I had found while with Ernest Adams, regular hours and routines didn't sit well with me for long. And again, just as it had at Ernest Adams, my mind was constantly racing, thinking of side projects to fill my restless evening hours. Mark, my colleague and partner-in-crime at the school, was a regular sounding board for all manner of bullshit business ideas. It was from one of these chats that Mark and I decided we had what it took to set up and run a successful baking consultancy, and so was born Krystal Klear Consultants, or KKC for short. This was 1992, so I can assure you the artful substituting of Cs for Ks was very much cutting edge at the time.

Dodgy name or not, the business did alright for a few months. I recall that our first consulting job was acting on behalf of an acquaintance from the soccer club I played for, a guy called Dave Callis. He ran a small independent flour mill (these still being the days when such a thing was possible and not all mills were run by huge conglomerates). Dave called us in because he was in dispute with a Greek bakery he supplied flour to. According to the baker, the flour was shit. Every time he baked pita with it, they went mouldy within a day.

Mark and I had never baked pita in our lives, but the KKC wouldn't earn a good name by turning down cases. We tested Dave's flour first; it seemed fine to us. As there was nothing apparently wrong with it, we then paid a visit to the Greek guy's bakery. The answer became clear when we saw how he took the pita from the oven and almost immediately packed it in cellophane wrapping, trapping the moisture that caused the mould. Our fee was earned by telling the baker, "Mate, you need to let the pita rest and cool down for a couple of hours before you pack it up."

Such easy money wasn't the norm, unfortunately. The baking industry in our part of the world was pretty small so, in truth, our consultancy wasn't much more than a couple of young guys trading basic baking advice to acquaintances and friends for modest fees every now and again. Still, it was fun, and it made us some extra pocket money. And at least it was a vaguely logical idea, which is more than I can say of another side business that Susan got me involved with: varnishing decorative bread.

Susan, like many a good English country woman, was the crafty sort, the type of person who knew how to arrange flowers and make potpourri. In those days, dried flower arrangements were all the rage in the crafting scene. From there, I suppose it was a short step to dried decorative bread. It is as bizarre as it sounds. Crafty people would get a basket and fill it with different types of dried bread rolls, sticking them together just so with a glue gun, maybe embellishing their arrangement with some sticks of cinnamon and nutmeg. These arrangements then lived life as a table centrepiece, destined to gather dust forever more. Of course, the fancier the bread rolls the better, so that's where I came in. Not only did Susan have me bake the things, but she insisted on me helping her varnish them too. Don't ask me how or why, but for a while there were plenty of people stupid enough to pay $3 per roll at craft fairs all around Christchurch. The trend disappeared as quickly as it had arrived, thank God — I was starting to lose brain cells from all the varnish fumes.

ERNEST ADAMS LTD

PRODUCT DEVELOPMENT
BAKER/PASTRYCOOK/FOOD TECHNOLOGIST

A VACANCY has arisen for a suitably qualified person to join the product development team based in Christchurch. The work involves the development of new products, redevelopment of existing products, and some staff training.

Extensive knowledge of bakery and related products is essential.

Applicants should be self motivated, be familiar with modern bakery plant, have good communication skills both written and verbal, and be able to work productively both alone and as part of a team.

Previous experience in product development is essential, and overseas experience is an advantage.

Please reply in writing with CV to:

R H Adams
Technical Director
ERNEST ADAMS LTD
PO Box 1006
CHRISTCHURCH

Applications close on October 14.

I began my technical baking phase doing research and development for Ernest Adams.

Ernest Adams was an established name in the business, making this job my first venture into corporate life.

When I was teaching full-time at the New Zealand Baking Training Centre at Christchurch Polytechnic, I got to mentor the New Zealand baking team. The team clinched victory at the Trans-Tasman Baking Trophy competition, just as the team I had captained a few years ago did.

My first baking consultancy business was set up with Mark Shrubshall, who was my colleague (and mentor) at the polytechnic.

Four

First Rising: Putting Into Practice + Fatherhood

Sideline projects like the short-lived consultancy and the bread varnishing were happy distractions from the daytime boredom at the baking school, but I still needed to figure out what step to take next in my career. It was John Kuipers, my partner in the butter flake rolls enterprise, who helped point me in the right direction. On hearing of my desire to leave teaching, he was the one who first raised the question, "Why don't you open your own bakery?"

It was a good question. I think for any baker, 99 per cent of them aspire to one day own and run their own bakery. I was no different. That aspiration had been vaguely lodged in the back of my mind since the first day of my apprenticeship. It had always seemed just a matter of time until it happened. I had been strategically building up my baking skills and learning all I could about baking as a business, arming myself for the day I would run my own operation, but I had never seriously sat down and carefully thought about the logistics of how I would get into the position to become a bakery owner, where the bakery would be located, and how the finance would be found.

John would guide me on the nitty-gritty of business acquisition when the time came but, first things first, we needed to find a business to take over. Most bakeries — especially in New Zealand in those days — tended to be family-run affairs, with the old man passing it on to his son. It was the nature of the industry. I didn't have this advantage of course, so I'd need to find a business for sale on the open market. This wasn't easy. Most towns only need so many bakeries, and when you discounted those waiting to be passed on to the next family generation, there weren't many left. John had put out feelers on my behalf and we quickly figured out that there was nothing suitable in Christchurch or in the surrounding area, so we'd need to consider farther flung fields. Despite New Zealand's large geographical size, news still somehow managed to spread quickly. In our industry, networks of flour distributors, equipment salesmen and assorted others involved in the baking business were a perversely efficient means of transporting gossip and information from coast to coast. This was how John got a tip-off about a place for sale in Dunedin.

Dunedin was a five-hour drive down the eastern coast from Christchurch and I knew it only as an old Scottish town where Otago university was. But with no other prospects on the table, Susan, John and I took a trip down one weekend to see what the story was. I wasn't immediately convinced by the town itself — it was, as I'd expected, just a rugged, middle-of-nowhere university town — but both John and I did have a good feeling about the business. Windsor Cakes was a traditional old-school Kiwi bakery that did takeaway only, but it did brisk trade and was trusted and well respected in the community. I could tell right away that there was potential. We didn't even look at the books on that first visit. We just watched the customers come and go, but instinctively it felt right.

After that, things moved fast. The old guy selling the business — Wally, an old-timer baker straight out of central casting — told us that he was looking for $150,000. This was steep, but we negotiated him down to a little over $140,000. Just like that, pending due diligence and some other paperwork, the skeletal terms of a deal were on the table. The problem was the $140,000 needed, which was a fuckload of money for a young guy starting out. This was going to require some financial gymnastics. I put in every cent I had of my own, which was barely $10,000. For the rest, I managed to convince my parents to help. As I had no assets, they agreed to use their house as security for a bank loan of $90,000, which I would be under the cosh (responsible) for. That was fair enough. On top of this, they stumped up $60,000 from their savings, which my father insisted that I paid back in five years at bank rates, so there was a 10 per cent interest to consider too.

This was a lot of money, and without it the opportunity would have passed me by, so I'm obviously grateful my parents came up with it. Sometimes, when people hear of this financial arrangement, they say things like, "Shit, Dean, that's a hell of a lot of responsibility to put your neck on the line for, especially with your parents so exposed." Well, true enough I guess — up to a point. They did show faith, but it was faith in the business proposition as an investment opportunity. Get it right: this wasn't a gift to their youngest son, propping him up to help him achieve his personal dream.

As was par for the course for my father, the whole financial arrangement became much colder and awkward than it needed to be. When I first mooted the idea of the loan to him, showing him my projections and assuring him I'd pay him back within a few years, he told me he'd think about it. A week later he got back in touch, asking me to come round to review a legal document his lawyer had drawn up in regard to the loan. My jaw almost hit the floor. Why did he feel the need for a lawyer to be involved? Did he not trust me?

I didn't have much choice in the matter. I went round to the house and sat at the table with my dad, painstakingly reviewing a 20-page loan legal agreement line by line. Below the layers of incomprehensible legal jargon, the basic terms were that I'd get my $60,000 loan, but I had to pay it back at full bank rates of interest after five years. Effectively this meant I'd end up paying $75,000. The lawyer went on to explain that as per the terms in the agreement, his client — my father — had the right to take my business and everything else I owned, bankrupting me in the process, were I to miss or default on any of the payments — standard mortgaging terms, I guess. Personally, I wouldn't seek interest on a loan I gave to a family member of mine but, okay, everyone's different.

In the end, the affair ended as bitterly as it had begun. As it transpired, I ended up selling Windsor Cakes after three years and was ready to pay my father back in full two years early. I remitted the remaining $20,000 or so to his bank account and thought nothing more of it until he demanded the unpaid interest for the remaining two years of the loan period. He even quoted the clause in the contract explaining that early repayment of the principal did not absolve me of the interest due over the full loan period. I knew of this clause, of course, but thought even my father wouldn't enforce it on his own son.

My father's position might have been understandable had I been planning to set up a new business from scratch — that would have been a risk, for sure. But this business was a stable and successful going concern. Even just toddling along at the current owner's tired and complacent way of doing things would turn a profit. This conviction didn't come from mere hopeful impressions, it came after we had undertaken a sustained period of due diligence, weeks spent watching the business in operation and poring over five years of Wally's old accounting ledgers. Having seen those, the pathway to repaying the loans was clear, it would just be a matter of time.

I quickly saw when flipping through these account books that Wally's P&L statements were in a bit of a mess. The top line was healthy — strong and steady sales month after month. But his profit margin was slim; his costs were too high. I drew up a forecast P&L statement of my own, using my own numbers, put it side by side with Wally's, and straight away I saw several glaring areas where costs could be trimmed and profits boosted. For example, he was spending 40 per cent on food costs, which was far too high. I could bring that down to 30 per cent easily. A similar thing with manpower. Wally had hired half the village — most of them were family friends — on too-generous wages. That would be easy to cut. The list went on. I didn't have a shred of doubt that I could quickly boost that profit percentage.

I recall going to see the bakery's belaboured accountant, a tired-looking guy called Tim. He was long used to working with bakers such as Wally — guys who didn't understand numbers or didn't care about numbers. Even if they did, they were too tired after a 14-hour shift to listen to his well-considered advice. I presented him with my forecast P&L and accompanying notes and asked if he'd mind looking over them. A little later, Tim called me back in, appraising me with a tilted eyebrow and the beginnings of a grin on his face.

"Well, my boy, you're a bit different aren't you?" he said.

"What do you mean by that?" I said.

"Dean, you're what I like to call an executive baker. Your numbers are good — spot on. You'll do well here."

Tim had worked with many bakers, but very few had an acumen for the actual business of baking. Most locked themselves in the kitchen and buried themselves with dough. These kind of bakers had to be dragged kicking and screaming to the accountant's office to go over the figures at the end of a month. Tim was right: I was different.

Business came to me naturally. It all started with a recognition of the importance — no, the absolute sanctity of the P&L statement. That piece of paper is your Bible, your Qur'an, and you live or die by your ability to read and understand one. I have lost count of the many brilliant bakers I have encountered throughout my life who just do not understand this. Whether embarking on a new venture or taking over a steady business, they will reliably proceed to fuck it up. And I don't really understand how.

To me, a P&L statement is just another recipe. We have a thing in our business called baker's percentage or baker's math. This is a formula that indicates the ratio of ingredients in a recipe relative to the weight of flour used. Flour is king, so it's always 100 per cent. If a recipe calls for 5 kilogrammes of flour, 2.5 kilogrammes of water, 0.5 kilogrammes of sugar and 50 grams of yeast, then in baker speak that becomes 100 per cent flour, 50 per cent water, 10 per cent sugar and 1 per cent yeast. Still with me?

This uses exactly the same principle as a P&L statement. Here, your sales become your flour, the 100 per cent. Everything else in your business is relative to this — ingredients cost, manpower, storage, marketing, overheads, whatever else. Last but not least, right at the bottom line of your statement is profit. This could be a healthy 30 per cent, or a piddling 2 per cent, all depending on how well you manage your costs, how well you balance the recipe. You'd be an idiot to try baking a loaf of bread with 130 per cent water to your 100 per cent flour — your loaf of bread will be shit. It's the same in business: if your costs have spiralled to 130 per cent of your sales, then you're screwed.

It might seem painfully simple — it does to me as I write this — but there remain plenty of people who don't get it. These are the people who wake up one day and think, "I'm feeling a bit tired. I think I'll hire an assistant to help me out." That's $2,000 added to the mix, which is perhaps 1 per cent of sales. But how does this affect the balance of your total recipe? If you don't know, then you are in trouble. Many business owners fail to keep on top of this. Many get seduced by sales alone, which might even be strong and healthy. A business might have sales of $100,000 per month for three months straight, with a profit margin of 15 per cent. "What a successful, thriving business I have," these owners think. So they start using more expensive ingredients and they add more staff — all without thinking about their P&L recipe. Suddenly, often without realising how or why, costs have climbed to outweigh sales. "But it was always so busy," they'll reflect sadly as they shutter their shop's doors for the last time. "I don't understand what happened."

They might call it baker's math, but to me it's business math. If you can read a recipe, you can read a P&L statement. It's not fucking rocket science.

With negotiations complete, due diligence done and finance secured, we signed the deal to buy Windsor Cakes in November 1993. Wally would keep things ticking over for a couple of months until January 1994, giving Susan and I a brief window to get our affairs in order and complete our move down from Christchurch. Oh, and there was also the small matter of our wedding, which we had in December, a week before we packed the van and moved to Dunedin. It was a simple but elegant wedding. Civil ceremony, flowers, garden party, family, dinner, speeches, cake — you know the drill. Married, boom.

This was an exciting time. Everything was happening incredibly fast. I had bought my first business, got married and, after moving down to Dunedin, Susan and I also bought our first home together. So now we had a house mortgage to service on top of the business-related repayments. Not once did I dwell on possible scary aspects of all of this — the mountain of debt, the huge responsibilities, moving far from our hometown. Call it the fearlessness of youth or whatever, but I only ever saw the positives, the opportunities. To be clear, I was making a calculated move down south with a strategy in mind. I wasn't planning on living in Dunedin forever. I was going to fix the business, make some money, pay off the loans and sell up — business, house and all. I set myself a five-year target to do this and told myself that when I made the return journey back north, I'd be doing so with a healthy bank balance and beholden to nobody but myself.

Like I said before, Windsor Cakes might have been a sleepy little business, but it was profitable. Upon taking the keys for the first time, I knew better than to rip everything up and start anew. In a small, close-knit community like Dunedin, for me to have introduced too much change to this beloved little bakery would have been tantamount to sacrilege. "Who's this cheeky young upstart," they would have asked, "coming down here thinking he's God's gift and undoing all of Wally's good work?" No, I knew better. Any changes and improvements would need to be introduced incrementally and stealthily.

This thinking is one of the reasons I didn't plonk my name on the sign from day one. As self-confident as I might have been, I was still sensible enough to recognise that the brand of Windsor Cakes meant more in this area than my personal name. I did add 'and Patisserie' to the end of it though, a small allowance I thought. But even that small compromise wasn't appreciated by the locals. "Who is this guy kidding with his big fancy words?"

You have to be careful in situations like this because even when changes you introduce are demonstrably good for the business, for many people any kind of change at all is anathema. I saw this when we tried to spruce things up a bit by repainting the walls. Of course, the locals soon let us know that they preferred the chipped and faded 20-year-old grey paint to our beautiful fresh azure blue makeover. Same thing with the countertop and display. Old Wally's was a horrible and old stained piece of white plywood with a thin sheet of cracked glass on top. This was one thing I wasn't going to compromise on. The very day I signed the papers to buy Windsor Cakes I picked up the phone and ordered an imported bespoke — and very expensive — Italian marble countertop and a stunning curved refrigerated display case.

Rather than compliment us on this luxurious new centrepiece, the regulars complained. "Oh, something's wrong with my bun. The cream is cold!"

At times like that it took all my reserves of patience to stop myself screaming back, "It's supposed to be cold, you old biddy!"

I didn't worry too much about these knee-jerk reactions. It's part and parcel of a cherished old business falling into new hands. The customers would come round after they had time to get used to it, and, sure enough, they did. Anyway, they were still buying our bread and putting money in the till, so they could grumble all they liked as long as they kept doing that.

The customer side of things would take care of itself in time, but I didn't waste a beat in getting things straightened out behind the scenes in the kitchen. Recipes and techniques were being followed there were last in fashion when bell-bottoms were. Out they went, replaced by new, tastier, more efficient recipes, most of them my own. Windsor Cakes was a very traditional bakery. Almost everything was being done by hand. This can sometimes be a good thing, but not if you want to make any money. So I brought in machines to speed up the dough mixing and rolling processes. That saved me at least 50 hours of labour cost a week.

I totally reorganised the layout of the kitchen. I noticed how Wally — who, we had agreed, would stay on for two months during the handover phase — would amble from his station all the way to the other side of the kitchen for a simple dash of sugar. This return trip took about 20 seconds every time, and he must have made it 60 times a shift. I said, "Wally, why don't we try just moving the sugar over here, right beside the workstation?"

That was one of many simple, incremental little changes that boosted productivity many times over, but poor old Wally just couldn't get it. Like a sleepwalker, he'd continue to trot over to the corner for his sugar, totally confounded for a few seconds when he couldn't find it in its usual spot.

Windsor Cakes, like many small town bakeries of its kind, tried to boost revenue by selling some product wholesale to surrounding shops and restaurants. I found the wholesale business to be a monumental pain in the ass. I always have. Even today I try to avoid it as far as possible. It's not easy balancing the twin demands of retail and wholesale from the same bakery. What if your shopfront product has been massively depleted by a crazy morning rush, but the stuff currently in the oven is slated for a wholesale order? What do you prioritise?

On top of the potential for operational confusion, it always just felt perverse that the very same loaf of bread fresh out of the oven was worth $6 to an over-the-counter customer who came to my bakery to buy it, but was worth only $4 after discount to a store that I had to drive 10 miles to deliver to their doorstep. And this is before thinking about the cost of packaging, or the time spent writing invoices and chasing for payment. Often I'd return from a 20-mile round trip delivering 20 buns and ten loaves for a mere $60 or so, only to be told by a colleague as soon as I walked in the door that ABC Convenience Store had called five minutes ago. Two rolls had been left out of their order, and they were insisting the missing rolls get sent over right away. Wally had set up dozens of these tiny wholesale accounts over the years. It was a messy, laborious, loss-making waste of time. I quickly set about dissolving the wholesale business entirely.

I was also determined to get to the bottom of a mystery that had been bothering me since I'd first seen the account ledgers. The stocktaking and sales figures didn't match up the way they should have, but there was no way to tell why until I had the chance to closely observe the daily ins and outs of the business for a few days to get to the bottom of it. Wally, like all bakers of his generation, was an inveterate workaholic. He started his days at 2 a.m. and baked non-stop until opening time and beyond. He ended his shift at 10 a.m. or so, leaving behind a mountain of stock for the afternoon's trading. Everything's normal so far. He'd go home and have a rest before popping back in later at 4 p.m. to check in on things shortly before closing. And almost every day, to his immense satisfaction, he'd find that 95 per cent of his stock had sold, that he'd judged the demand perfectly once again.

If it was truly the case that his product was selling out practically in its entirety every day, then the takings should have been much higher. But Wally, an old-school baker to his core, didn't have a grasp on the economics of his business. He just baked as much as he could, left it to the customers to buy it all, and whatever in the till at the end of the day was what there was. As far as he was concerned, if he was selling out of such a large stock every day, then his business couldn't be better, could it?

The reality was quite different. What was happening was that after Wally went home at lunchtime, the product remained piled up, selling steadily, but slowly, over the course of the afternoon. Far too slowly to get through all of it. Come 3 p.m., with only two hours of trading time left, the staff would panic and slash prices for everything — half-price loaves, three-for-two deals on cupcakes, buy-one-get-one-half-price on bread rolls, you name it. And this happened every day. Customers aren't stupid, so they just waited for the daily panic to set in and did their shopping in the late afternoon every day. So the product was selling, but it was selling at bullshit prices.

Poor Wally, none the wiser, popped in every day like clockwork just as the mad rush died down, saw the empty displays and set about baking exactly the same amount of product for the same thing to play out all over again the next day.

Correcting this wasn't difficult. All I had to do was bake two-thirds of what was normally being baked and ensure the staff sold it at its proper price for the whole day. It took a while to explain to them that selling less product would be a good thing; it was about protecting the margins. It is better to sell $100 of product and make $20 of profit than it is to sell $200 and make $5 profit, I told them. Naturally, this wasn't a popular move with customers or staff. Customers were pissed that they now had to pay fair money for their bread and the staff were pissed because the customers started giving them grief. So be it — my business wasn't a charity.

Yet even this didn't totally resolve the stock and revenue imbalance. I delved into things further and found that pilferage was rife. Again, poor Wally was far too trusting of his long-time staff and so-called friends, who had clearly gotten into the habit of taking home a couple of loaves of bread for the family each day. They even raided the lettuces and tomatoes brought in for the sandwich bar. Cute little Johnny and Emily, kids of the counter staff, would pop by on their way home for their free slice of chocolate cake. It was a free-for-all.

Needless to say, the Windsor Cakes staff I inherited didn't last long. Then again, neither did their replacements, nor the ones after that. I was hard on my staff in those days — in hindsight, probably too hard. When we were wrapping up the business a few years later, Susan looked up from the books at me and asked, "Do you know how many staff you went through?"

"Nah, go on, tell me."

"35, Dean. 35 staff in three years."

It dawned on me then: well, no wonder I was so fucking tired the whole time. I could never keep a full quota of staff on board at any one time. The problem was that I demanded very high standards from my staff members and didn't have much patience when they failed to meet them. At the time, I genuinely couldn't understand why such standards were out of reach because to me what I was asking seemed easy. Nor could I understand how my staff weren't as driven as me — how could they just stroll out at closing time without a care in the world when we had so much work to do for the next day?

I was also quick to anger when someone made a mistake. "What do you mean the hot cross buns are fucking burned? Why do you think I bought ovens with a fucking timer on them if you're not going to use it, you idiot? Tell you what, as soon as you've scraped those trays clean, get your coat, fuck off and don't come back."

I was too wild and reckless in those days. I was still young and I think I forgot that I was a better baker than most — not everyone I worked with was an Apprentice of the Year. I couldn't reasonably expect them to be of the same technical standard as I had reached. Same thing with the passion. Of course the bakery was going to occupy my every waking thought, and of course I was going to work 16-hour days to make things better. It was my business, my livelihood. But for the 22-year-old cashier on minimum wage, what did he stand to gain — in the short-term at least — from doing overtime and stressing himself out? It was naïve of me to think regular staff would sweat as much blood as I would for my business.

I've mellowed a lot since then and learnt to allow some leeway, but I will never apologise for setting and keeping high standards. Look at Wally. He was probably like me when he started out. But, over time, the pressure of insisting on the utmost high standards and the constant churning of staff got to him. Maybe he started to think he was being too hard on staff and asking too much of them. "It's only a burnt tray of buns after all," he might have started thinking. "Sure, the guy has a habit of coming to work late, but he's a nice fella and he needs the job. I can't sack him. This bread doesn't taste great but I suppose it's not bad. It'll do. Too much hassle to make a fresh batch now."

This kind of thinking is a slippery slope. And fuck me, I wasn't going to let myself become an old, fat, washed-up baker whose 'friends' are stealing his lettuce behind his back.

As well as the back-office operations, Windsor Cakes also gave me a valuable crash course on front-of-house sales and marketing. Retail is detail. Creating delicious product was the easy part, something I could do in my sleep. It was at the shopfront where I started to learn most new things, how seemingly imperceptible details helped move my goods. I came to understand that display is everything. I learnt the importance of angles, how to place the products in rows on slightly tilted shelves and always below — but not too far below — eye level. Glass shelving was a must. All of this creates visual depth, giving the customer the best view of a wider range of goods. Lighting is crucial too. There is no point having a beautiful arrangement if people can't see it properly.

Simple stuff, you'd think, but when frantically busy bakers barely have time to take a piss, then you can see how this level of granular detail escapes their attention. Sometimes shopfront staff spend a lot of time arranging their displays, ensuring everything is just right, perfectly symmetrical and everything from their point of view. Remember, they stack the display from behind the counter, but the customer isn't seeing what they are. Even today I have to constantly remind staff to get out from behind the counter and look from the outside, from every possible angle a would-be customer sees things. It all makes an important difference.

The bedding-in period at Windsor Cakes took a few months but we gradually chiselled out a workable routine, built a somewhat settled staff and had a regular flow of customers. That being said, it was a hard grind. Ultimately the business was going to live or die on the volume of sweat Susan and I put into it, and we both did our fair share, believe me. The long shifts baking the product were obviously not a surprise to me, but I also had to factor in all the gritty little shit that you needed to do to keep a business going. In those days you didn't get deliveries from every supplier, so there were daily round trips to the grocers for vegetables for the salad bar, long drives to the cash and carry for bottles of orange juice and takeaway boxes. There was all the maddening people management stuff; a pimply teenager works two shifts and thinks he deserves a raise. The phone never stopped ringing — usually some pen-pusher was on the line, wanting to remind me a flour payment was a day overdue. In the middle of service the electricity might go out. Cue frantic calls to the power service provider to find out what the fuck was going on. It was never-ending.

Susan, to her credit, flung herself into all of this with me. More than she needed to, honestly. She was a godsend on the accounting and admin side of things. She was the one who ensured the flour bills did get paid, one day late or not. She kept the supplier orders organised, scheduled deliveries, wrote up the accounts at the end of the day. She really grafted. It got to the point where she started coming in with me at 2 a.m. to open up the shop. I tried to dissuade her but there was no telling her. I'm sure most of it was a genuine desire to help me, but there was also part of her that was afraid to stay at home all day bored and listless. I can understand that.

All this hard work and stress did make our domestic life tough, especially when we started opening on weekends and became a seven-day-a-week business. We spent most of every day together but in a demanding work environment. We barely had a minute together in relaxed circumstances. The business was consuming every waking moment. Naturally, there were arguments and tears, real strains on our young marriage. But we kept going — what else could we do?

Being owner of Windsor Cakes enabled me to become a member of the New Zealand Baking Society, kind of a guild for bakers all over the country. Many trades and industries have such societies — plumbers, bookbinders, carpenters, whatever. They are useful for networking and staying abreast of the latest news in your area of business. I joined the Baking Society primarily so I could enter the New Zealand Baker of the Year competition, which was organised by them and open only to members. These competitions were important for brand building, as I've explained before, so I was keen to get back into the competition circuit again and show everyone who was boss.

Being a member of the Baking Society was one thing. Any baker could become one by filling out a form and sending in their membership fee. I was after more than that; I wanted some actual influence. The New Zealand Baking Society, like all societies of its type, was operated by an executive committee, or the ExCo. The Baking Society ExCo was a snake pit of petty politics, dominated by an old-boy network going back decades, where the same seats were held by the same doddery flour-dusted cronies year after year. Innovation and renewal were not words known to these types. It's not that they didn't have new blood join the ExCo every so often — they were forced to — but the implicit rule was that if you got in, you followed their way of doing things. It had worked for the past 60 years after all, so why change things?

I was determined to get myself on the ExCo and drag these old-timers into the 21st century, which was rapidly approaching. It was 1994 when I stood up at the Baking Society's AGM and announced my candidacy to join as an ExCo member. Of course, you couldn't just rock up from nowhere and do this. Someone on the ExCo needed to second your motion and there was no chance of that unless you had all your ducks in a row long in advance. I did — I had spent weeks silently campaigning, making calls and using all my powers of intrigue and persuasion. My votes of support were already secured. In truth, it would have been tough for them to turn me down anyway. My name had been known in the industry thanks to my role at Ernest Adams, my teaching days, and my achievements as an apprentice, so it's not like I was a non-entity. Sure enough, the vote went in my favour and I was made the New Zealand Baking Society's youngest ever ExCo member.

Fuck me, did they come to regret that. With membership safely secured, when the next New Zealand Baker of the Year competition rolled around, I entered in every single category. I was determined to prove myself as the best baker in the country, which I was convinced I was. I was especially pumped up for this because this was my first year competing in the big leagues. Apart from my contributions to Rangiora's competitions all those years ago, my previous competitions, whilst prestigious, were at the apprentice level, when all the competitors were still juniors. This would be the first time I went directly up against seasoned adult bakers, using all my own recipes and techniques. Given my natural highly competitive nature, there was a lot riding on this for me. All of this helps explain my anger at the total shitfest of a competition that followed.

I had already seen from several encounters with the Baking Society in the past, and especially in the past few months as an ExCo member, just how amateurish and lazy they could be. But I was still shocked at some of the bullshit their organising committee threw up at this competition. Battle lines were drawn in the very first category, 'Chelsea Buns', I think. I saw the committee members handling and arranging other bakers' buns themselves, absent-mindedly placing them askew on pathetic looking white doilies.

"Hang on," I said, "aren't points being awarded for presentation in this category?"

"Er, well, yes, Dean. Presentation is a criteria for all categories, I believe."

"How can you give points for presentation when there is no bloody presentation being done? It's just you lot moving the stuff from the bakers' boxes onto a bloody paper doily!"

The lady I was speaking to was just a volunteer, so it wasn't her fault. This was on the Baking Society and how they'd drawn up the judging criteria. Still, I wasn't going to take this lying down. The idea that they could give points for presentation when the bakers had zero input in setting up their displays was obviously bollocks. I had prepared all my products with presentation very much in mind. I planned on competing like I had at college level, full of innovation and artistry. I had brought custom-cut mirrors, props, and labels and cards with bespoke graphic designs. I found the head of the organising committee and told him in no uncertain terms that I was to be in the room for the setting up of each and every one of my displays. I would either set it up myself or, if that wasn't allowed, I'd stand behind the volunteer and direct their every move until my mirrors and props were positioned at precisely the correct angles.

Needless to say, when the head honchos in the ExCo got wind of this, that the young upstart Brettschneider, voted onto the ExCo only recently, was throwing his weight around, creating trouble, slowing down the schedule and upsetting the poor volunteers doing the set-ups — well, they weren't happy. "How dare this little shit try and buck our system? We've had the same judging criteria for the past 60 years, yet he's the only one to ever have a problem. Who does he think he is?"

There's no doubt that this cost me. When the results for presentation in each of the 26 categories were read out, I received my fair share of golds, but nowhere near as many as there should have been. Evidently, the judging panel was making a point. It was embarrassing for all involved, to be honest. Some bakers who got gold ahead of me actually came to me to apologise. There was no escaping the absurdity of the whole thing.

The whole competition weekend proceeded like this: ill-considered judging criteria were followed by bizarre judging decisions, with grumblings and frostiness in the air every time I aired my grievances, wondering what the hell was going on. There was an evident anti-artistic snobbery in how things were being judged. In particular, anything innovative or new I put up was invariably marked lower than the most bog-standard traditional versions. It was clear that I was being perceived as a show-off. But this was no rinky-dink village fête. This was our country's premier baking competition for professionals. It should have been treated as the ultimate testing ground for baking skills and techniques.

Despite this, they still couldn't ignore my technical skills completely, so I chipped away, picking up gold medals and points, swimming against the tide all the away until the final category, 'Black Forest Gateau'. All I needed to win the overall competition was a bronze, so I knew there was no way I could lose from here when I compared my work to those of my competitors. I had really gone all out with mine; it was one of the best things I'd ever created. I was genuinely proud of it. I made use of all of the techniques I'd learnt overseas and baked it based on the most authentic, delicious recipe I had been given by an actual Bavarian baker. Presentation-wise, it was stunning, if I do say so myself. I was practically rehearsing my winner's speech in my head already.

The problem was that the winner of this category was being voted for by the public. Don't get me wrong, public votes are great in some contexts. The public are ultimately your customers and their views are the most important to listen to for any business owner. But this was a professional competition, and the public weren't experts on baking styles and techniques. I had prepared my gateau for the eyes and assessment of baking professionals, so obviously I went for a level of artistic sophistication in line with this. Had I known the public were judging it, I would have gone for something more down to earth. But that's beside the point: the final category in a professional baking competition should have been judged by professional experts.

On top of this, layeration was listed as one of the key judging criteria — layeration being how well defined and uniform the different layers inside the gateau were. But during the judging, they didn't even cut the fucking cakes! How can you judge on layeration when you don't look at the bloody layers? Farcical.

There were a few hours in between the setting up of the displays and the final prize announcement at the award ceremony that Sunday evening. I used that time to seek out anybody of influence on the organising committee I could find to try and rectify what I perceived as these obvious abuses of justice. I found some sympathy, but not much. It was too late in the piece anyway. A few choice words were left for all involved.

By the time it came to the ceremony, I could see the writing on the wall. I could have cried when they announced the winner of the 'Black Forest Gateau' category, a more bog-standard cake you would have struggled to find. It wasn't even authentic. But it's what the public were used to buying from their local bakery for their little Timmy's 6th birthday. People like what they are familiar with. I was stitched up. I didn't even get the bronze medal I needed to win Baker of the Year, and so I went home empty-handed, but with a head full of the abuse I would give the Baking Society at the next ExCo meeting the following month.

Sparks flew at that meeting. I was still seething at everything that had gone on at the competition. I told all the crusty old committee members that they should be ashamed of themselves for running what should have been our country's premier professional baking competition like a village fête. There was more professionalism in the college and apprentice competitions.

"Anyone who has ever rolled a piece of dough knows that the baking I put out at that competition should have won," I said. "I was robbed. You know it and I know it."

Of course, they accused me of just being sore that I didn't win. That was bullshit. I told them I would happily have lost to any baker with better product than mine, but that demonstrably hadn't been the case. As the custodians of our ancient trade in New Zealand, the Baking Society had the responsibility to promote the highest standards of professionalism in their events and competitions, and they should encourage innovation, technical aptitude and creativity, not actively seek to inhibit it like they had with me.

All of my arguments hit a nerve. I think most knew I was right, but they couldn't admit as much and thereby admit to their own incompetence. Whatever the merits of my views, there was no rowing back on the fact that I was by now very much identified as the troublemaker and upstart of the baking industry in these circles. All because I had the temerity to try and improve things. Admittedly, I could have been more political about it. Played a longer game where I accepted losing some battles to win the war. That is how I would play it today, but I was young then, emotional and ambitious. I tended to react when people tried to fuck me over.

Despite a very awkward and rocky relationship with the rest of the ExCo, I stayed on for two years before finally resigning after one argument too many. I wasn't going to give the other members the satisfaction of forcing me out sooner, so I stayed on and made improvements to things where I could. I like to think that my volcanic reaction to the Baker of the Year competition really helped tighten up and professionalise the criteria and judging methodology for future iterations, so bakers who came after me should have benefitted from that.

Throughout those tempestuous battles with the ExCo, one committee member who really stood by me and helped smooth over some of the bigger problems was a man called Paul Hansen. I don't use the term mentor lightly, but he was one of the few in my life who really had a huge impact on me, professionally and personally. Paul was the Godfather of New Zealand baking, the kindly old sage who could silence a room of boisterous argument by calmly delivering his opinion. Once he had spoken, the discussion was over and judgement had been passed.

I think Paul and I hit it off because he had a mischievous streak in him too. Perhaps he saw me as something of a wild child incarnation of himself. Paul, especially in his older years, definitely wasn't the type to rock the boat himself, but he loved to do so vicariously through me.

Paul and I would often chat long into the night on his front porch and there'd be a glint in his eye when I'd tell him of my plans to really go after the ExCo at the next meeting, to really call them out for all their crap.

"Now, Dean, I'm not going to tell you what you can or can't say, but I agree with you that they do need to be called to account."

When the meeting came round and my comments invariably stirred strong reaction, it would be Paul who interjected, "Now, now, let's all take a deep breath. I don't think Dean meant any offence. I'm sure what he meant to say was..." Later, on his porch, we'd be in fits of laughter recalling the events. Paul would say, "Did you see how red Ian's face got when you called him corrupt? He didn't take that well, did he! Good on you, Dean."

On 29 October 2015, Paul passed on, but his legacy in the Kiwi baking world will live on for a long time to come.

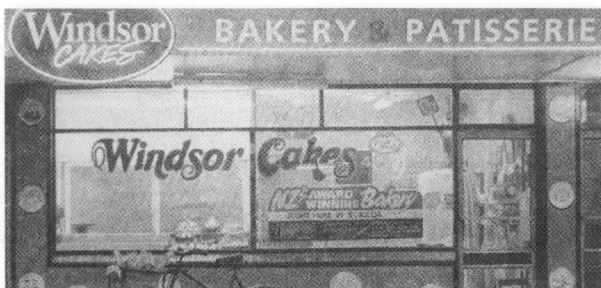

Windsor Cakes — the first bakery that Susan and I purchased together.
I wanted to learn how to run a business.

Taking over and running a business was a lesson on
considering customer insights while looking at the
bigger picture and trusting my gut.

An old friend once said that even if I
were having the toughest working day
of my life, I should always smile and say
I'm doing great. There I was, smiling!

My first sign-written car, which I had done six weeks before we took over
Windsor Cakes. It got people talking and asking what I was up to.

The headlines should have read 'Baker prepares for battle', as I had been about to take on the old guard of the New Zealand Baking Society.

A bread display celebrating the New Zealand Baking Society, which was founded in 1967.

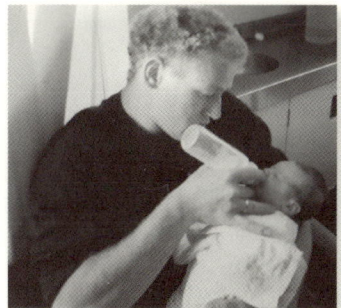

25 January 1996. Jason popped into our lives. He's a cracking son, and both Susan and I are so proud of who he has become. He will go on to greatness!

Having some father and son time. 23 years on, Jason and I still enjoy hanging out.

Five

Knocking Back: Corporate Development + Publishing

My involvement with the Baking Society — rocky ride though it was — was another important strategic step for me. Industry players tended to take notice of the goings on with the Baking Society, noting who the movers and shakers were, and where the power lay. Being an ExCo member helped get me more media exposure for Windsor Cakes. Consequently, suppliers became more flexible with their discounts and faster with their deliveries. I was well aware of all these benefits and was more than happy to use whatever advantage I could for the betterment of my business.

And business was good. So much so, in fact, that when I looked at the accounts one day, about three years after taking over, I saw that my initial five-year forecast had been achieved already. There was little left to pay back from both the bank loan and the loan from my parents, and the business had plenty of cash in the bank. Taking the finances out of it, I realised too that my main learning and development targets had also been met. I'd taken over a business, learnt the ins and outs of daily operations, increased the customer count, and developed a hell of a lot of marketing, branding and retail skills.

All of which meant that when a company called Goodman
Fielder came calling in 1996 with a very enticing offer, I was ready
to sit down and listen very carefully. Goodman Fielder was a giant
of a company, manufacturing and distributing baking ingredients
and a wide variety of other goods across Australia, New Zealand
and Asia Pacific. These guys were in the big leagues. Their pitch
to me was straightforward. "Join us up in Auckland and make
us the number one baking ingredients supplier in the southern
hemisphere." (They were number two at the time.) "You'll be one
of our youngest ever senior executives, you'll have a company car
and you'll fly business class on all of your overseas trips. Oh, and
we'll pay you a shit load of money too."

This was quite an offer for a 27-year-old and after three years
of the daily grind at Windsor Cakes, it sounded very good to
me. It would be a relief to hang up the apron, give the 2 a.m.
starts a break for a bit and get back into the corporate swing
of things again. Perhaps if one or more of the elements of the
whole package had been missing, I would have had more of a
dilemma, but as it was, this offer ticked every box: big name
company, exciting job role, career advancement opportunities,
good money and perks, based in a cool and bustling city. I didn't
take too long to accept their offer.

A buyer for Windsor Cakes was swiftly found; it was a more
attractive proposition now than it was when I first took it over. It
still boasted the customer base and good name of the Wally era,
but I'd improved the product, boosted profit and modernised the
whole set-up. In fact, I probably sold it too cheaply in my rush
to get up to Auckland. My accountant looked like he wanted to
punch me when I told him I'd sold it for only $50,000 more than
I had paid for it. I was happy enough with that. It was enough

to pay off our remaining debts and the moving costs, and we'd be in a good position when we started our new chapter. By this point, 'we' meant more than just Susan and I. We would be making the move north with our beautiful six-month-old son, Jason, in tow. Susan and I had both long known that parenthood was on our horizon. It was just a matter of when. We took the decision to start trying for a baby in 1995, about over a year into our Windsor Cakes life in Dunedin. The time felt right. Our world together was very small, revolving around the business, our home and one another. There was little time for a social life, so it felt natural that we focus on building our domestic one, even though we were so young.

Seeing your firstborn enter the world is just one of those things that words can't do justice to, so I won't waste time trying here. Suffice to say, it was one of the happiest moments of my life. Some say that having children turns their whole world upside down, that it changes everything. But for us, we found ways for Jason to fit into the life we had before he came along. This resulted in him becoming a real fan favourite with our customers and staff, because as an infant he'd spend many hours with his mum and dad, propped up on the counter in the bakery. Susan was a great mum straight off the bat, and I think I did my fair share too. The 2 a.m. feedings were often my job — life as a baker had made me immune to waking at ungodly hours anyway.

Of all the decisions we made during this part of our lives, this was definitely one we got totally right.

We had barely set foot in Auckland before we immediately knew we were in the right place. The whole place had a different energy to Dunedin. It was on a different scale. To put it in perspective, Auckland, with 1.5 million people, was ten times bigger than Dunedin. This meant longer high streets, a plethora of shopping and dining options, theatres and music venues, you name it. With the company-sponsored car and the AMEX card thrown in there for good measure, a whole new world of lifestyle opportunities had opened up to us. Of course, with a newborn in tow, we couldn't immediately avail of everything Auckland had to offer, but it was good to know it was there!

Thankfully, my Goodman Fielder pay packet was enough to support Susan staying home as a full-time mother, which was great. Susan and I agreed that it would be good for Jason to have his mother with him throughout his early years, and it was a relief to remove the burden of work from Susan. She had been putting in a lot of work at Windsor Cakes, which would have proven unsustainable for much longer now that Jason had joined us. This new domestic arrangement suited all three of us better.

The new job hadn't come totally out of the blue. Even during my busiest times at Windsor Cakes I didn't let myself get buried below mounds of flour and disconnected from the wider industry. I continued to stay in touch with all of the contacts, friends and acquaintances I had met over the years. Such contacts could range from Tesco's global head of in-store baking to the biggest flour and ingredients merchants in Europe. I always innately understood the value of these relationships. Whether it was a quick five-minute phone call, a pop-in visit during a trip to London, or even a handwritten Christmas card with greetings for their family, I made sure I reminded them all that I was alive and kicking, ready for a chat if anything ever came up.

And it was through this channel that the Goodman Fielder job came up. They had heard lots of good things about me from influential people in my network and figured I was exactly the kind of character they needed. They were determined to become the number one baking ingredients company in the southern hemisphere and to do that, they wanted a maverick, someone not afraid to push boundaries and think outside of the box. Clearly my reputation had preceded me.

The actual job title was National Technical Support Manager. It was a wide-ranging role, not easy to define really, but generally speaking, I was responsible for developing new products, managing the test bakery, training customer service and sales teams, and handling our biggest VIP accounts. And even all of those responsibilities didn't cover my input on branding and marketing too. Fair dues, as you don't get the big pay packet and the car for doing nothing. Bring it on, I reckoned. The more responsibility the better.

They said they wanted a maverick and it didn't take me long to assure them they had found the right man. As part of my job, I was often sent to international trade fairs to scout out new products and industry innovations. These trade fairs were a real eye-opener. I learnt a lot not just in terms of products, but also in the art of salesmanship and presentation. The Europeans and Americans were miles ahead of us in that regard. They made us old-timey Kiwi companies look like country bumpkins in terms of how we marketed our stuff.

Inspired by what I had seen overseas, I was determined to make a bang back in New Zealand when the next conference came around. In New Zealand trade conferences, typically you were stuck in a massive, soul-destroying warehouse space, parked at your little table amid 30 others and left to hope that you somehow got noticed by the people that matter. For this particular conference in 1997, about a year into my spell at Goodman Fielder, the organiser had come up with a Parisian boulevard theme, mandating that everyone had the exact same little round table, complete with table umbrella. They provided detailed brochures outlining the precise dimensions of each exhibitor's space. Uniformity was key, presumably so that nobody had an unfair advantage.

Fuck that. I was going to make our display stand out.

The classic Italian cake panettone was the big baking trend of the time and we had recently developed a great new panettone premix to capitalise on this. We were launching this product at the conference and were banking on it being a big hit. As soon as I saw the sketches and dimensions of the standard display tables that the organiser sent over, an idea immediately sprung to mind.

A proper panettone has a round, cylindrical base, with a protruding dome-like top and a base wrapped in a paper cup. So when I looked at the organiser's photograph of the round table and umbrella, what I saw was the base of a panettone (the round table) and its characteristic dome top (the umbrella). We lined the table, its sides and the umbrella with superimposed images of an actual panettone, giving the impression of a life-sized cake, with the top cut off and raised to let people see 'inside'.

It looked very cool and, needless to say, very different from all the surrounding Parisian café table clones all of our competitors were stuck at. They could only look on in horror and envy at the insane foot traffic we drew to our life-size panettone. We racked up sales for our premix beyond even our wildest hopes. Of course, all of our competitors moaned, "You can't do that! That's not fair!"

The conference organisers were summoned to adjudicate in the matter, whereupon I quickly pointed out that we had the same round table, chairs and umbrella as everyone else, just as the rules dictated. I had been through the guidelines very carefully, I told them, but I didn't see anything that outlawed adding some creative flair to make the set up resemble a popular Italian Christmas cake. The organiser could only shrug and slump off, the enraged competitors chasing after to harangue him. The poor guy must have been thinking, "I'm not getting paid enough to deal with this shit."

When I got back to Auckland and told my boss what had gone on, it took him about five minutes to stop laughing. When he did, he said, "Bloody hell, Dean, you really took me seriously when I told you to ruffle some feathers, eh? Good man, that's exactly the kind of thing we brought you in here for. I just wish I was there to see their faces."

Goodman Fielder was, in many ways, the perfect fit for me. And I don't say that lightly. I could not have dreamt up a more ideal role for my character and skill. It was the perfect balance of technical baking, sales and marketing, branding and networking. I had a big hand in all of these things, but never were any of them a singular focus, which would not have worked as well. This multi-hatted role really allowed us to do things faster and with more purpose. We were a massive company, but in my department at least, there was mutual trust for us to make quick, purposeful decisions. For example, I would go to big key account meetings with the sales team. In the past, when the big buyer asked if a particular product could be tweaked — to make it gluten-free, for example — in time for the Christmas season and with no significant increase in his cost, the sales guy wouldn't have a fucking clue. "I'll have to go back and discuss that with the baking team," he'd say. "Let us work out a production schedule and the budget and I should be able to get back to you in two or three weeks."

By which point, the buyer would probably have already gone to our competitor and placed his order with them.

With me in those meetings, such things didn't happen. Now when someone asked about a gluten-free version, I understood exactly the technical nature of the question. As soon as the words had left his mouth I would immediately calculate how many tonnes of gluten-free flour we'd need, the name and number of the supplier I'd call, the price I'd barter him down to and the exact date he'd have it sent to our warehouse. I'd then factor in the time we'd need for testing, then the manufacturing, packaging and delivery.

Now, the buyer had his answer in a matter of seconds, not days or weeks. "Steve, that won't be a problem at all. What is it you need — 200 tonnes? We can have that manufactured and delivered to you by the first week of November. Cost-wise, well, we need to do some math homework but I can assure you it will be no more than a 2.5 per cent increase on the cost of the regular flour. But I'll get you a precise figure tomorrow."

With that, the deal was done.

It was around 1998, 1999 maybe, when it struck me that despite the fact I was a big name in baking industry circles, with a great job and unparalleled CV, and was widely known and respected, the public at large didn't really know me from Adam. That in itself was no problem, but when I looked around my office at the bulging files of creative and delicious recipes I'd come up with, or when I received rave reviews at baking competitions from judges telling me a particular bread was the best they'd ever tasted, it struck me that us industry players were all just talking in an echo chamber. We were demonstrating new tastes and techniques all the time, but sharing them only with each other. I wanted to get that know-how into the public domain, and there was no better way to do that than putting it all in a book.

In those days, food and the media were not bedfellows like they are today. Cooking has now gone mainstream in a big way. Every other TV channel has a cooking show on every second of the day. Back then there was no *The Great British Bake Off* and the bookshop shelves weren't heaving with culinary books. Nobody had a clue who Jamie Oliver was. It was a nascent market and even in the subcategory of culinary books, general cookbooks ruled the roost. Baking cookbooks, by comparison, were an afterthought. The view was that only baking professionals bought such books. They were too technical for the home baker and, anyway, home bakers stuck to their own tried and tested family recipes.

This was the scene I faced at the time, but rather than being intimidated by these challenges, I thought it showed that the market was crying out for a book that shattered the existing conceptions of what a baking cookbook was. And with little competition in the market, particularly in New Zealand and Asia Pacific, any such book would have significant first mover advantage. Thankfully, when I took my ideas to an independent and forward-thinking publishing house, Tandem Press, they agreed with all of this.

My vision was to produce a book showcasing the best of Kiwi baking. It wouldn't just be me. The idea was that I'd curate and present recipes from many of the best bakers around the country, calling in favours and contacts to ensure their participation in the project. This really would be a compendium of the best of New Zealand baking. And it would be a beautiful, highly visual book that was immediately accessible to the general public. Baking books of the time were more like technical manuals; you were lucky if they even had sketches, never mind photographs. My book was going to be different. I wanted a stunning, full-colour studio photograph to accompany every recipe, and dynamic shots of the bakers in action too. Candid, natural. A section at the front of the book would act as a (highly detailed) crash course in baking fundamentals, carefully laying out basic techniques to give every reader the grounding they needed before trying any of the recipes. This is how a lot of baking books of the time failed — and still do, in fact. They just plonk in the recipes without explaining techniques such as how to knead properly or how to correctly age your dough. This results in many home bakers trying a recipe once, fucking it up royally, throwing away the book and warning their friends not to waste their money doing the same. "Bloody recipes don't work," they'll say.

Tandem Press, run by a lovely salt-of-the-earth husband and wife team, loved all of this. They were fully on board. "But," the publisher said, "Dean, I know you're trying but there's still too much jargon in your recipes. And you're a B2B name, not a public one. Little old Mary Smith will see your name and picture on the book and think, 'Who's this fella to tell me how to bake?'"

He reckoned, as it was, they could sell maybe only 500 copies within baking industry circles, but we needed to think in terms of 10,000 copies and beyond to cover the costs. His solution? "How about you give Lauraine Jacobs a call? Here's her number."

I didn't know Lauraine at all at the time. I only knew that she wrote for *Cuisine*, a magazine that was hugely respected and boasted a massive international circulation. She was the High Priestess of New Zealand food writing. Tandem's idea was that she could make my recipes and technical writing more accessible, as well as act as the brand name on the cover to provide bookshelf credibility. Her connections would be valuable in helping to bring in some big name bakers as contributors and her influence would guarantee post-publication press and publicity. It all made very good sense. Lauraine and I had a good chat about the project, and it was good to hear how genuinely excited she was to work on a baking book of such ambition. Almost all of her writing up to that point had been focused on general cooking.

Lauraine and I worked very well together. I faxed over my recipes and notes to her and she sent back her revisions and comments to me for approval. Lauraine did interviews with the other contributing bakers and we worked together on the recipes they submitted. I pored over them for technical integrity and Lauraine made sure a home baker would be able to actually read them. The publisher invited me to many of the photo shoots and I helped art-direct to ensure the photographs were as stunning as I'd envisaged from the beginning.

And so it came to pass, in 2000, *The New Zealand Baker: Secrets and Recipes from the Professionals* was published, my very first of 16 (and counting) books. The final product was everything I hoped it would be. It was far more impressive and glamorous than any other book beside it on the bookshop shelf. The partnership with Lauraine, as the publisher had understood from the outset, was key. Between us, we ensured the information and recipes in the book were of the highest professional standard, but were still understandable to any Tom, Dick or Harry at home. All of this, together with the beautiful visuals, resulted in a genuinely brilliant book, one I remain very proud of today.

Thankfully for me, and the publisher, New Zealand's food critics agreed with my assessment. Tandem was only a small family-run press but they were canny marketers and knew their business. With Lauraine's help, they secured reviews and features in practically every media outlet in New Zealand and plenty more in Australia, seemingly all of which were glowingly positive. The publicity drove customers to the bookshops and the book flew off the shelves, so much so that it needed several reprints in its first year of publication alone.

It wasn't all glamorous radio slots, book signings and glossy magazine features. A lot of grunt work went into making the book a success too. As a first-time book author with a personal brand to build, I was happy to do whatever was asked of me. So I dutifully packed my car boot full of books and drove around making direct sales to friends and family. I painstakingly went through my Rolodex and shamelessly hawked the book to associates I hadn't spoken to in years. I did baking demos in front of five grannies and their dogs at village fairs — whatever it took to get the book into people's hands.

It was pleasing to know the book was selling well, but it wasn't about mere sales figures for me. To be frank, even 20 years ago when the publishing industry was in far better shape than it is today, my annual royalties weren't much to write home about, so I wasn't in it for the money. Plus, some of the shittiest books ever written have become bestsellers, so sales alone can often be a poor indicator of quality. Far more important to me was how people reacted to the book. Was it as good as I hoped it was? Were people actually using it? The initial sales and critical reaction suggested yes, but it wasn't until after all the publicity died down and the book continued to sell strongly through word of mouth alone that I knew for sure it was a true hit. Affirmation was complete when the book promptly picked up two prestigious awards. It came out on top in the 'Best Photography' category at the Gourmand World Cookbook Awards in France in 2000, and a year later it took home the Golden Ladle for 'Best Soft Cover Recipe Book' at the World Food Media Awards. Known as the Oscars of the food business, the latter award was particularly sweet and it marked the culmination of a crazy first foray into the world of publishing.

Tandem Press didn't let Lauraine and I rest on our laurels. The ink on the first book was barely dry before we were signed on for our second book, which was published in 2001, called *Baker: The Best of International Baking from Australia and New Zealand*. The concept for this was essentially the same as the first book, but with broadened horizons to get some of our Aussie friends in on the act too. This widened scope of contributors was important; if book one was about me establishing my name at home in New Zealand, then book two was about me announcing myself on an international scale. And it worked. With its focus on Australian baking, the book led to a raft of Australian media reviews and commentary, which brought us a huge new audience and opened doors for international co-publishing deals. *Baker*, like its predecessor, was a success in both bookshops and awards circles, picking up a Gourmand World Cookbook Award in the 'Best Bread' category.

Even I couldn't have anticipated just how influential and successful my first two books turned out to be, I definitely wasn't arguing. *New Zealand Baker*, in particular, proved to be a real game-changer. Publishing a book in the first place was, in large part, about making a name for myself among the general Kiwi public, or at least with the small part of the public that gave a shit about baking. The book totally nailed that objective. So much so, in fact, that the public came to not only regard me as a good, trustworthy New Zealand baker, but also think of me as the 'New Zealand Baker', just as the title of the book said.

Our foresight and timing had been so good, and the wave of publicity that followed so strong, that practically overnight I had been appointed New Zealand's baker laureate. Now when other cooks or bakers wanted an endorsement for their book, they sent requests to me. If a lifestyle radio or TV show wanted to feature a baking tips segment or a live demo, I was the one they called. Newspapers and magazines invited me to submit columns, labelling me the country's best baker. The words 'baking', 'New Zealand' and 'Dean Brettschneider' become synonymous.

That space — 'New Zealand Baker' — was valuable real estate just waiting to be grabbed, and boy did I grab it. Today, almost 20 years later, there is far more competition for the title, but I'm still holding on to it. To illustrate, literally as I write this, I have just taken delivery of *Kiwi Baker at Home*, a new book of mine published to coincide with the TV show *The Great Kiwi Bake Off*, on which I appear as the main judge.

None of this happened by chance. I knew exactly what I was doing when I proposed that book title all those years ago. I was determined to position myself as New Zealand's only baker worth listening to. I repeated the phrase over and over in all the interviews I did subsequently, almost giving the journalists no choice but to refer to me as the 'New Zealand Baker'. I myself added the tag to my own letterheads, name cards and email signature. I built a crappy little website and bought the domain nzbaker.co.nz. I even bought number plates for my car that read NZBAKR! I wasn't shy about taking the title if no one else was going to lay claim to it. Ever since, I've been disciplined about continuing to appear in the public eye, lest some cheeky so-and-so tries to sneak in and steal my crown. If I find myself overseas for too long, I'll make some calls back home, publish a new book, or get myself on a TV show — whatever it takes to remind everyone who New Zealand's national baker is. I'm not going anywhere.

Establishing my position as the 'New Zealand Baker' was one thing, but building a personal brand beyond New Zealand's borders was a different matter. They might not have topped the New York Times Best Seller list, but my books did make a modest splash overseas, particularly book two, *Baker*. It was a first attempt at cracking Australia, which would be an important stepping stone into the international markets. Initial results couldn't have been much better: the book was well received, got plenty of publicity, sold well and was nominated for awards. As hoped, the book helped open doors into circles I otherwise would never have had access to in New Zealand alone. Which is how I came to know Rick Stein.

Off the back of book one's success, Tandem Press had no problem selling the Australian rights of *Baker* to an Australian publisher, so when the book was published in 2001, plans were put in place to do a book tour over there. While these plans were being made, we also heard that *New Zealand Baker* had been nominated in the 'Best Soft Cover Recipe Book' category at the World Food Media Awards. The ceremony was to be held in Adelaide just before Christmas at the end of 2001. Perfect. Arrangements were made for a book tour to promote *Baker* at events in Melbourne and Sydney before wrapping up in Adelaide, where I could both promote the new book and attend the World Food Media Awards weekend.

An energetic and brilliant young publicist called Sarah handled all of the nitty-gritty of these arrangements for me. Sarah worked for the Australian publisher of my book, who also held the territorial rights for Rick Stein's books. In a fortuitous coincidence, Rick was in Adelaide at the same time as I was. He was in town to promote a new TV show and attend the awards ceremony, so the opportunity arose over the course of the weekend for Sarah to introduce us.

We didn't actually meet at the awards ceremony — in the end I had to miss that to rush off and catch a plane to London to continue my book tour. But we spoke at the launch event for *Baker*, which had been integrated into the award weekend's programme. The event was well attended as Sarah had done a good job generating interest and corralling attendees from her network of contacts, but I must admit to being a tad star-struck when I glanced up during my baking demo to see Rick Stein watching on intently. He patiently hung around to the very end of the demo and book-signing. After Sarah introduced us, we struck up a lively conversation.

I was humbled when Rick told me how much he enjoyed *New Zealand Baker*. Sarah had sent him a copy the year before and since then it had been the baking book he found himself turning to the most. Ordinarily, I took such compliments with a pinch of salt as people tend to exaggerate out of politeness. But Rick was known for being such a straightforward person and for being so passionate about food. He really seemed genuine. If there was any global celebrity chef in the world likely to know about and use a relatively obscure baking book from New Zealand, it was Rick Stein.

We talked for a long time about all manner of things. He was tickled when I told him that Susan was a Cornish woman, hailing from his neck of the woods. When I mentioned that I was skipping the awards ceremony to finish the book tour in London and spend Christmas with Susan's family, he said, "Well, that settles it then. Let me have the number you'll be using in the UK. You must go down to Padstow and teach my chefs how to bake bread properly. I'll be back home a few days after you. I'll give you a call when I'm back."

True to his word, that's exactly how it played out. Contact details were quickly exchanged, emails sent and plans put in motion. And so it came to pass that a couple of days after Christmas, Susan and I found ourselves leaving her family and the turkey leftovers to catch a train down to Padstow for me to spend a week working with Rick's baking team in his bakery. When the work was done, New Year's Eve was spent in the pub celebrating with Rick and his wife, Jill, where we all proceeded to drink a glass or six too many glasses of champagne. As the wine flowed, Rick and I concocted ever more ambitious plans for a cross-continental business empire. Together, we could rule the world!

Emboldened by the drink or not, there was genuine substance in some of the partnership ideas. And as I'd quickly come to learn, when Rick says he'll do something, he does it. My kind of guy. So come 2 January, the after-effects of a two-day hangover still throbbing at the back of our heads, Rick and I stepped into the numbingly cold English winter looking at possible properties in the Padstow area for us to launch a bakery partnership.

I had seen how skeletal Rick's baking operations were when I was doing the consulting work. He only had a tiny deli and a poky industrial bakery supplying his restaurants. That got my mind whirring, and given Rick's passion for food, it didn't take a lot to enliven his enthusiasm. The idea was to set up a simple, but high quality patisserie. My know-how and recipes, his name and local influence. We had even discussed a name for the enterprise — Baker at Stein's. We might only have known each other for two weeks, but we were deadly serious about it. I even had Susan make enquiries with the airline to find out how much it would cost to postpone our flights for a few days so we had more time to confirm some more details.

Unfortunately, the plan fell apart as quickly as it was set up. The momentum dissipated a little bit after I returned to New Zealand, and a jealous executive chef of Rick's took the chance to throw a spanner in the works, telling him there was no need and no resources to diversify into baking at that time. Plus, was he sure he could even trust this random Kiwi guy who had shown up from nowhere? The idea was canned, or so I thought. I allowed myself a rueful smile when 18 months later I picked up a food magazine to read all about Rick Stein's exciting new bakery venture — Stein's Patisserie.

There is no doubt that this was a total rip-off of my idea, but I let it go. It was one of those things. My personal and professional relationship with Rick had been fruitful in the year and a half since our first meeting. He helped make connections for me and provided kind words and reviews for my books. I tried to do the same for him, not that he needed it. Bearing grudges now would do nobody any good and it wasn't Rick's fault that he was being fed such poor advice. I occasionally pause to think about what might have been had things played out differently, but it's hard to get too regretful about it. I don't think winter in Padstow would be much fun.

I was still with Goodman Fielder during all of the activity surrounding the publication of my first two books, their launches and publicity tours, and Rick Stein and all. And in fairness to my bosses, they were very supportive of all of it. They trusted me and let me do whatever I wanted so long as I kept up my levels in the day job, and I made sure I did that. I didn't neglect a single thing. In fact, I probably overcompensated and worked even harder than I ever did before the books came out. If I had something book-related to do in the afternoon, then I came to the office at 4 a.m. to keep on top of everything, completing a full day's office work before any of my colleagues had even arrived. Plus, the top brass knew what they were getting when they hired me. They brought me in for my innovation and initiative, so to have inhibited me in my publishing endeavours would have been a betrayal of that understanding.

In any case, it was good business for Goodman Fielder to have a somewhat well-known name in their ranks. They benefitted plenty from my burgeoning public profile. Any time I appeared on a show or in an article, Goodman Fielder's name appeared in my bio. I recommended Goodman Fielder products in my recipes, and I included the company logo on the acknowledgements page. At exhibitions or meetings, clients often said things like, "Ah, the New Zealand Baker himself! I read about you in *Cuisine* magazine just last week." It was an effective icebreaker to precede multi-million dollar contract discussions. I gave copies of my books to all of our most important customers, which tended to leave a stronger impression than a dog-eared name-card. I would often meet important food industry figures at book events, a launch or an awards show, and such contacts occasionally turned into new business for the company. Nobody recognised this better than the former CEO of Goodman Fielder New Zealand, Colin Wise. He had my back every step of the way.

Not everyone in the baking world was so gracious. I had to deal with a fair degree of tall poppy syndrome. Some petty colleagues were resentful of the flexibility shown towards my working hours and leave-taking, choosing not to recognise that this 'flexibility' meant I had the pleasure of slogging in the office for hours before they clocked in, or on weekends while they were home relaxing. Many of my professional peers were no better. Jealousy was rife. I had, after all, been plastered all over the media for the past two years as "New Zealand's number one baker", which tended to grate on competitors. Many of the bakers who actually contributed and appeared in the two books even refused to buy books from me at a wholesale discount — they weren't being called for interviews or being offered publishing contracts, so why should they support Brettschneider? Needless to say, I didn't have many customers among my old friends at the Baking Society either.

I didn't let such small-mindedness get to me. I was too busy achieving things.

1996. I joined Goodman Fielder to head their technical support department and help boost them from number two to the top spot in NZ for bakery ingredient supplies.

Celebrating my first book in 2000, I had no idea back then that I would write more than one book!

The World Food Media Awards are the food and drink publishing world's equivalent of the Oscars. Here are my two Golden Ladles for *The New Zealand Baker* and *Taste*.

The many charity books I get involved in all become part of Baker & Cook and my team are always happy to help out and learn along the way. People with passion always give time and make time.

I think "a guy from nowhere but with many influences" is a pretty accurate summary of many successful individuals.

I've published 15 cookbooks to date across the span of 19 years.

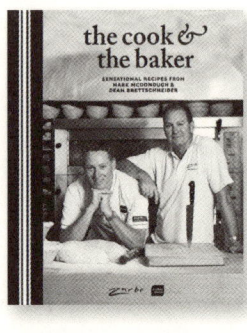

A TREASURY OF
New Zealand Baking

Nestlé
HOTTEST HOME BAKER

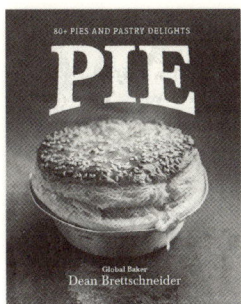

80+ PIES AND PASTRY DELIGHTS
PIE
Global Baker
Dean Brettschneider

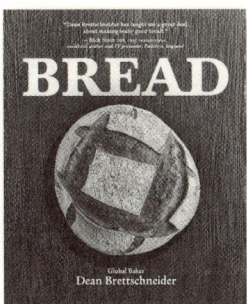

BREAD
Global Baker
Dean Brettschneider

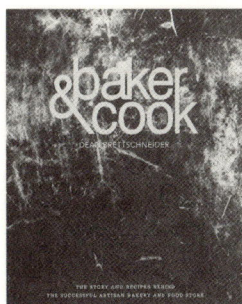

baker & cook

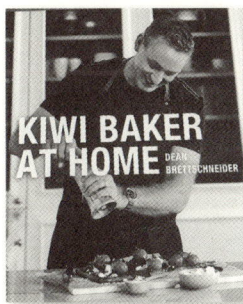

KIWI BAKER AT HOME DEAN BRETTSCHNEIDER

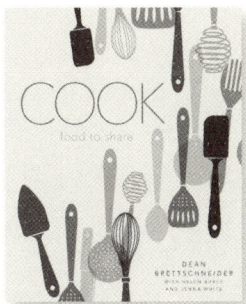

COOK food to share
DEAN BRETTSCHNEIDER

Six

Shaping: Global Baking

I had seven great years at Goodman Fielder before that chapter came to an end in 2002. There were no real push factors driving me out, although there was an irritating power struggle with an ass who headed the Sydney department. He tried for years to relocate me to Australia, simply to make his life easier at the cost of making mine more difficult. I refused to give in. This small fracture aside, things were otherwise going so well at Goodman Fielder that I would only have considered leaving for a unique opportunity that truly excited me.

That came in the form of a new business venture in London. Colin Wise, formerly the CEO of Goodman Fielder and a friend of mine, had left the company to pursue other interests. There was plenty of money in the social circles he hung around in, and plenty of it in the pockets of a man called David Gaze. Colin informed me that David had bought a thriving B2B bakery from a Turkish family in a hotspot location in London. Patisserie Organic, it was called, and he could think of no one better than me to run the place. "Here we go again," I thought.

David was a charismatic guy and sold me on the idea during an impassioned discussion over coffee. "Dean, there's nobody on the planet better suited for this than you. I've read all your books. I love your style, mate. London's going crazy for anything organic these days. Let's get you on a flight over to check out the place."

A matter of days after that, David was proudly showing off his investment to me on a chilly London afternoon. To be honest, I was underwhelmed. It was much smaller than I had expected, and the interior fittings and finishing had seen better days. The location wasn't much to shout about either, parked in between two greasy takeaway joints under the arches as it was, far from any significant foot traffic or Tube stations.

David's enthusiasm was an effective smokescreen, however. "I can see what you're thinking, Dean. Don't worry about those old cupboards and the walls. A contractor has already been hired to sort that. I've put aside a big budget for renovation. And this area might not look like much now, but people around here think of it as the next Chalk Farm. Trust me, this is London's next trendy spot. This will just be the start. I've already earmarked three or four other locations for the next branches once this place gets up and running." On top of this sales pitch, the terms of his offer were enticing too. He was making me CEO and I'd earn a 20 per cent ownership stake in the business after two years. All our moving costs would be covered as well.

I took the offer. I flew back to New Zealand to serve my notice at Goodman Fielder, packed up the family and two months later, Susan, Jason and I touched down at Heathrow ready to start our new life in the UK. We might as well have stayed on the plane and gone straight back to New Zealand. Taking this job proved to be one of the rare misjudgements I've made in my career. From the start, nothing seemed to go as planned. The promised renovations never happened and the area itself remained derelict and devoid of customers. I might have been called CEO but, really, I was just the baker. A return to the back-breaking 16-hour days, what I thought I'd left behind when I sold Windsor Cakes. But unlike then, now I was merely an employee and not even my own boss. It quickly began to feel like a step backward.

There were a litany of other irritants and problems. David had reached some kind of mysterious arrangement with the previous owners so that they hovered around the place like a bad smell for months, creating an awkward dynamic and disputes over who was actually in charge. Most of the old staff were kept on too, some of whom were lazy and unreliable, and the rest totally useless. David, for his part, was nowhere to be found most of the time. If I called him to discuss an urgent problem at the bakery, he fobbed me off, busy as he was skiing in the Alps or playing golf in Spain.

Six months in, it was clear that the situation was untenable. I told David I couldn't go on and that I planned to return to New Zealand. That wasn't something I took lightly. David had placed his hopes — and a fair degree of cash — on me, and now the partnership was dissolving before it had really even started. But the situation was what it was and there was no point in dragging it out any longer. David wasn't happy, of course, but I did the right thing by him and stayed on until he found a replacement for me. And I paid him back every cent of the money he put towards moving me and the family over from New Zealand. We parted on okay terms.

The Patisserie Organic experiment wasn't a total failure. I was proud of the product we were making and the focus on environmentally-friendly, sustainable eating was far ahead of the curve. Few people talked about gluten-free allergies and other healthy eating fads in those days. Its problem was that this was a hipster place that came around 10 years before actual hipsters existed.

But, overall, I have to admit, taking the job and making the move was a mistake. For one of the very few occasions in my life, I allowed bold promises and optimistic conjecture to cloud my judgment. I should have simply trusted what I saw with my own eyes. Someone might try and spin a story that a shithole is actually a rough diamond, a characterful joint merely in need of a lick of paint and brimming with potential, but, really, it's just a shithole.

When it became clear that things weren't going to end well in London, I started making calls to my contacts in the European baking world to see if there might be something of interest. One such call was made to Peter De Jager, a big cheese in the Amsterdam office of BakeMark International, a leading global manufacturer and distributor of baking ingredients. Peter asked me to pop over to see him in Holland to discuss a possible role in their new Asia Pacific headquarters, which would soon be opening in Shanghai.

BakeMark was part of a sprawling conglomerate called CSM, which owned countless baking manufacturers and distributors. Any product, item or service related to the baking industry you can think of, CSM owned the businesses behind them. CSM was Goodman Fielder on steroids, and BakeMark was one of their biggest brands, so it was a good fit for me.

A job offer came quickly. The idea was to try and centralise the representation of all of CSM's European brands within the Asian market. CSM might have owned 60 different companies in Europe, and until then each of these companies flew their salesmen over twice annually to see their Asian buyers. It was inefficient and also led to CSM's own companies fighting each other for the same customers. CSM wanted to set up a single sales and account team in Shanghai to represent the entire suite of CSM services and products, enabling six people to do what 60 were doing before. BakeMark was the name given to this new office for these functions and I'd be joining that team as Technical Account Manager, Asia Pacific.

So after a pretty dispiriting six months in London, we packed our bags to make the return journey to New Zealand, arriving back in late 2002. BakeMark didn't send me to the Shanghai office right away; it wasn't fully up and running yet, so for the first few months in the job I operated from a base in Auckland. My base was only a nominal one. I spent only one week per month at home, while the rest of the time was spent travelling all around the globe to innumerable CSM-owned companies, discussing orders, shipping times, prices, import and export issues, and God knows what else on behalf of our Asia-based customers.

In an unfortunate bit of timing, my job appointment also coincided with the onset of the SARS crisis, which effectively grounded travel in and out of China. There was a period of three months or so when CSM issued a directive that banned all staff travel in and out of the country, so that pushed back the full-time move to Shanghai further still, and led to me spending much of my first year in the role travelling to the CSM offices dotted around Europe rather than Asia.

Finally, after several months practically living on aeroplanes, the SARS situation calmed down enough for me to finally set up base in a company-owned apartment in Shanghai. This would have been in the middle of 2003 or so. I moved over by myself initially. My work travel schedule had kick-started a period of time when Susan and I drifted apart. The distance and time spent away from each other was a heavy burden on us emotionally, and also created circumstances that led to me making some serious personal fuck-ups along the way. Susan and I agreed that she and Jason would stay in New Zealand while I found my feet in China first. We weren't giving up on our marriage by any means, but it would take time and space to iron our issues out. To try and do so while dealing with the stress of moving continents with a young child in tow would not have helped with that.

I had long been a frequent global traveller but this was my first taste of living in Asia. Shanghai intoxicated me from the get-go. It is a city that assaults all of your senses: the blaring traffic, the shrill calls of street hawkers, the pungent-smelling wet markets, the sparkling stratospheric skyscrapers, the neon lights of the dodgy karaoke bars, the alien tastes and textures of its food. Shanghai was a sprawling metropolis of more than 20 million people. Every street felt alive with energy, activity and possibility. I was determined to leave my own little imprint on the place.

Both the book *Wolf of Wall Street* and its movie adaptation painted a rich picture of the egregious excesses of Wall Street in the 1980s, and while my time in Shanghai didn't quite reach those depths, it wasn't a million miles away from it either. The first two years, in particular (2003–2005), were a constant adrenaline rush that it was like being on drugs (although there were never any actual drugs involved, I can assure you, unless we're counting caffeine pills and paracetamol).

Remember, the whole reason I was there was to consolidate a wide suite of Europe-based companies and their offerings for our customers in Asia, so there was no concept of regular office hours. All day and all night my mobile phone buzzed with calls from clients, colleagues, bosses, partners and shippers. I thought of my day in three parts. In the morning and early afternoon I dealt with Asia. Late afternoon to dinner-time was Europe's turn. When they were dealt with, I might have time for a dinner appointment with a key account before the American offices opened and presented me with their problems. Once the Americans were appeased — my mobile phone by now drained of battery — I'd rejoin my clients in the cocktail bar for a drink and delicate contract negotiations. Then, I'd be home at 1 a.m. with the alarm set for 5 a.m. for the cycle to start all over again.

I didn't resent this — far from it. The surges of adrenaline were addictive. Each new mini crisis became a perverse pleasure. The problems brought with them a familiar, nauseating anxiety every time, but I had the blissful relief of resolving the issue to look forward to, and that always outweighed the temporary stress. And I can't lie; it was nice to know how important I was to so many people. With my phone constantly ringing, people from all around the globe seeking my advice and assistance, it felt like I was at the epicentre of the baking universe. I liken it to being at the controls of a Formula One car on a wet circuit — you can navigate the course perfectly safely with your foot firmly on the throttle, but God help you if you try and slow down. The real danger comes when you apply the brakes.

This was also an era when Western mother ship companies were totally naïve about the countries they were setting their offices up in. Expat contracts were gloriously over the top in a bid to entice their executives to these 'hardship' postings in far-flung Asia. That meant business class flights, unlimited entertainment and expense accounts, personal drivers and indecent pay cheques. I lapped all of this up. Even better — nobody in China could reasonably be expected to pronounce 'Brettschneider', so I became "Mr Dean". Soon enough, there wasn't a maître d' in town who wouldn't rustle up a table for two at a second's notice for me. "No reservation, Mr Dean? No problem. Just a moment, Mr Dean."

Don't get me wrong — this was still all in the name of work. As the most senior Westerner in the Shanghai office, I become an important connection to some of the very biggest global companies operating in Asia, including Starbucks, so I was frequently wining and dining the big shots and testing the company credit cards to their limit. Fun was being had, but business was being done — big business. BakeMark couldn't have been happier with the work I was doing, and with good reason.

The day job alone — regardless of how intense it might have been — was never going to be enough to keep me satisfied. By the time 2005 came round, the SARS scare had abated and things with BakeMark were going great guns. Susan and Jason had moved over to Shanghai to join me too, so things were also settled on the home front. But even five minutes of relative peace and quiet was anathema to me, leading my mind to start firing with new ventures to explore. It was time to introduce the name Dean Brettschneider to the wider Shanghai public.

One entry point to doing this was through a partnership with the renowned chef David Laris. Like me, David arrived in Shanghai in 2003, albeit with considerably more pomp and ceremony than I had. His restaurant, Laris at Three on the Bund, was one of the hottest tables in town, and deservedly so. I could testify better than most as to the quality of the food he was putting out. I was there at least once a week with clients. It was contemporary Western fine dining at its best.

After yet another fantastic meal there one evening in 2005, David and I were introduced and before we knew it, we were engaged in a two-hour-long conversation. And similar to my earlier experience with Rick Stein, my first chat with David proved that there is little need for small talk between true, passionate, business-minded foodies. I told David I was impressed that his restaurant did all of its own baking in-house. You could really tell that his breads and pastries were delicious. "But," I told him, "it could still be better."

Rather than being offended, David said, "Oh? Tell me how."

From that first meeting, David and I quickly became good friends and it took only a matter of months for us to establish a working partnership. Further to his renowned restaurant, David also had a chain of delicatessen and cafés in the city, called SLICE Delicatessen & Café. We struck a deal for me to operate a micro-bakery within that, called Dean Brettschneider at SLICE. There was little cash involved in this deal, except for a modest consultation fee. Ultimately the business was run by Chinese owners — even David was only a figurehead really — so this project was all about personal branding and the opportunity for opening doors and creating connections. There were fewer better ways of getting my name and products out there than having them printed and publicised alongside one of the hottest chefs in Shanghai. It was a win-win for everyone involved and worked out well.

Of course, I fully disclosed this side project with BakeMark, just as I always did in the past with any extracurricular activities

I pursued while in the employ of someone else. BakeMark was fine with it — initially, at least. I was more than pulling my weight in the office, so they were happy to let me build my personal brand however I wished. They, like Goodman Fielder before them, wisely deduced that there could only be positive side effects for them from me building a personal brand in the public arena.

It was a good thing BakeMark was open-minded about my side projects, because I ended up publishing prolifically while in Shanghai. It was around the same time as the foray into SLICE that I received a call from my old friends at Tandem Press. They had recently been bought over by the publishing giant Random House and they wanted to know, since it had now been several years since my first two award-winning books, wasn't it about time we did another? Never comfortable out of the limelight for too long, I was well up for it. Time to get the band back together. Lauraine Jacobs was duly called, we found a brilliant food photographer called Aaron McLean and we all set to work.

This third book was *Taste: Baking with Flavour*. My first two books featured bakeries and personalities alongside the food, but this time we doubled down on more than 50 dessert recipes, all of which were my own creations. As the title made clear, this book was all about taste. The desserts were the stars and Aaron's stunning photographs really did them justice. The formula worked and for the third time out of three, the book became an award winner. In fact, this one did the double, winning in the 'Best Desserts Book' category at the Gourmand World Cookbook Awards, and scooping another Golden Ladle for 'Best Soft Cover Recipe Book' at the World Food Media Awards.

Two years after that, in 2007, came my fourth book, titled *Global Baker: Inspirational Breads, Cakes, Pastries & Desserts with International Influence.* This was an important one, as it marked a new direction in my personal branding. If my earlier experiences in New Zealand had been all about establishing myself as the 'New Zealand Baker', then my years in Shanghai helped change my perspective and widen my horizons. My recipes and business approach, even parts of my personality, had now been shaped by international and multicultural influences. With that came what seemed to me a natural personal rebranding to 'Global Baker', a term that's stuck with me ever since.

Global Baker was a great book, actually, if I do say so myself. It remains one of my favourites. As it was my first book without Lauraine, I enjoyed letting my own writing hand run free. The book went way beyond a mere recipe book, really, incorporating travelogue writing and brilliant candid, documentary-style photography from Aaron. It even came with a DVD of me in action, demonstrating techniques and recipes.

A third book in three years arrived in 2008, born amid a storm of problems elsewhere in my life (more on that later). Not content to stop at the SLICE collaboration, I mooted the possibility of a book collaboration with David Laris. He told me it was always something he wanted to do but had never had the time or know-how to realise his ideal concept. No problem, I told him, I'll help you get it done.

The end result was a book called *The Menu.* This was no mean feat. Until today it remains the only book David has done! David's concept was ambitious, shall we say. It was a collection of 15 five-course fine-dining menus designed and presented by David and me — not something a casual home cook would be able to easily replicate, to be honest. The book performed only modestly in the market, which I had an inclination would be the case, but I was keen on the project mostly to cement my relationship with David. Royalties may have been light, but you couldn't put a price on the spin-off benefits of working with a world-famous chef like David Laris.

Like *The Menu*, the micro-bakery in SLICE wasn't a big money spinner, but it was a calculated effort to get my name mentioned in the circles that mattered in Shanghai. Almost like clockwork, this worked exactly as planned and led to a huge opportunity presenting itself. Sometime in 2007 I received a call from a man called Craig Willis. He was a group chef at a popular chain called Wagas and he wanted me to supply breads and pastries to him. I agreed to explore it further and soon enough, Craig had arranged a meeting with the Wagas owners, John Christensen and Jackie Yun. There may have been two of them but it was clear straight away that John was the real driving force.

Wagas was well known in Shanghai by then. The chain was a Western-style, modern casual sandwich, salad and coffee place. Today, such places are everywhere, but John had been one of the first movers to push such a concept in China. He set Wagas up in 1999 and it rapidly vacuumed in customers from Shanghai's large proportion of upwardly mobile, aspirational, trend-conscious urbanites who had money to spend. By the time of our meeting in 2007, Wagas had mushroomed to a dozen stores and was expanding fast.

"Dean," John said, "I was checking out the competition and picked up one of your baguettes at SLICE. Delicious. Tell me, how do I get you to set up a similar deal with me at Wagas?"

I was straight with him and explained that my presence at SLICE was a branding tie-up. I wasn't an owner or shareholder so there wasn't anything tangible I could sublicense to Wagas. But I was obviously hooked by the prospect of working with such a successful and thriving chain that I couldn't let this slip. I said, "I'm sure we can work something out, but to help me get a picture, what kind of volume do you need?"

"Well, it is variable of course, but on average, we need about 300 baguettes per day, a similar number of sliced white loaves…"

That was a pretty good number. "I see, so that's 300 units, divided by your 10 outlets, so we're talking 30 units per store daily. Okay, a micro-bakery arrangement could just about work, but it would be a stretch, I'll need to—"

John smiled before gently interjecting, "No, Dean, it's 300 per store per day. And that's just baguettes and loaves. I also need croissants, bread rolls, Danish pastries — you name it."

This, as I explained to John, was a whole different kettle of fish than simply setting up a small time micro-bakery within his existing outlets' kitchens. "John, with that kind of quantity, you'd be far better off setting up your own bakery."

With that suggestion, Baker & Spice was born. And a huge can of worms was opened with it.

Immediately entranced by the idea, John suggested to meet the following week to brainstorm ideas over a beer. I came prepared; I had thought of little else in the days since, unfurling in my head all the ideas and concepts I had developed over the years. As an industry insider, I had a front row seat to the burgeoning casual lifestyle dining scene. With Wagas, John had already aptly demonstrated the market segment I was after was out there, so I set out my vision for why an artisan bakery concept would work just as well as, if not better, than Wagas' light dining concept.

Beer in hand, John watched on closely as I animatedly scribbled out the whole concept and business plan on bar mats and napkins. It would be a complete artisan bakery and food store that sold great breads, pastries, cakes, cookies, granola, jams, chutneys, wine. The bakery would have a clean and sleek design, with marble countertops and large angled glass displays. There would be simple menus using elegant fonts, printed on good quality paper. Customers would sit at polished wood tables, sipping high quality coffees served by young, knowledgeable and confident staff.

I explained to him how the mechanics would work from a business point of view. Baker & Spice's bakery would obviously serve its own shopfront, but would also act as a central bakery kitchen to serve the baking needs of all the Wagas outlets around the city. I wrote down simple cooked food menu ideas that would complement the baked goods and spoke more on how we could market and brand Baker & Spice to ensure we captured both sit-in and takeaway customers.

It was a sure-fire hit, and John knew it. I could practically see the dollar signs spinning in his eyes. Discussions continued over the next few weeks but as the business proposal became more robust and talk turned to ownership terms and such, I became a little anxious over the tenuous position I was in. John and his business partners were big fish in Shanghai. They had deep pockets, influential connections and a keen understanding of how to navigate the administrative labyrinth of business in China. I, frankly, had none of those things. What I did have was the creative concept and business plan. The problem was, so now did John. I'd given him the whole thing scribbled on beer mats, after all.

I was relieved, then, when John agreed to do the right thing by me. First off, he made sure I was paid a healthy upfront consultancy fee for kick-starting the whole project and providing the creative blueprint. Second, he accepted my proposal for a 20 per cent ownership stake in the business, on the mutual understanding that I would stump up the cash for my share when I could in two years time. Unfortunately, for a number of reasons, cash was particularly tight for me at that time, or I would have given it to him there and then. We drew up what I thought was a formal agreement between us that outlined the terms. In essence, it named me and John as co-creators and co-owners of Baker & Spice, with my 20 per cent ownership stake to be ratified after two years, when I would purchase the shares at set-up cost (i.e. not market value). The document was signed, dotted and stamped. Deal done.

How naïve I was.

As expected, Baker & Spice was a success from day one. There were long queues on opening day and they seemed to only get longer after that. Beyond the sales at Baker & Spice itself, the bakery was also supplying all breads, pastries and desserts to the Wagas empire, and because my product was far superior to what Wagas had before, all of those outlets reported spikes in turnover too.

I was far from a silent partner. Whatever free time I could squeeze from my schedule, I was down there, speaking to the staff, discussing the products, solving problems, bartering with suppliers, discussing the P&L with the general manager. As far as I was concerned, Baker & Spice was my business and I was just doing my bit as business partner. I even roped in my old photographer friend, Aaron McLean, and starting working on a new book to promote the store.

As the months went by, business continued to boom. Yet as sales increased, so too did the distance between John and me. He became cagey when I asked him for certain business details, and also passive-aggressively told me to spend less time at the bakery. "You needn't bother yourself so much, Dean. I'm sure you are busy with BakeMark. Let the staff do their jobs."

About a year after Baker & Spice opened, I sensed I was about to get screwed over. I told John that my financial situation had improved and I was ready to exercise my option to buy my 20 per cent of the business early. "I can sort the financing out in a couple of weeks. Shall we call a lawyer to help draft the partnership agreement?"

John's face blanched. He started nervously scratching his head and avoided eye contact. I knew what was coming. "Ah, Dean, about that. I have spoken to the other partners about this a few times over the past few months but it's more complicated than we thought. You see, the business is a Wagas-owned entity, whose shares are already all owned. I've really tried but I don't think there's a way to get you in on this."

"John, we have an agreement. And you know better than I do that it would take five minutes of form-filling at City Hall to register Baker & Spice as its own private business, so don't try and bullshit me."

"Well, the Wagas lawyers asked to see that agreement. They had a close look and they reckon it doesn't represent a formal business agreement. It wouldn't stand up; it's more of a memo—"

"Oh for fuck sake, John. Really? The least you could do is to not hide behind pathetic excuses like that."

With that, it was over. I had somehow become a 100 per cent creator but zero per cent owner of a business that was printing money. Needless to say, I didn't take this treatment well. Maybe John's lawyers were right; it's quite possible the agreement wasn't worth the paper it was printed on, but that was far from the point. We could have written up the terms on a piece of toilet paper for all I cared. The paper was just a symbol of our man-to-man agreement. When I do business, I do so with total transparency and integrity, something I have quickly come to realise is far from the norm, especially when millions of dollars are involved. With John's contacts in Shanghai, there was no point fighting the issue. Apart from the fact that he was so well connected in the business community and was lawyered up to his eyeballs, John's father-in-law also happened to be Shanghai's former chief of police. Yeah, I didn't stand a chance.

My experience with Baker & Spice was a painful but valuable lesson in doing business at the top table. Looking back now, there were several steps I could have taken to protect my interests better. I could have held back more of the creative concept, I could have fought harder to raise the cash for the 20 per cent stake from the outset, or I could have had a lawyer vet the agreement John and I made.

Should have, would have, could have. It's all moot now. I'd be lying if I said it didn't hurt to see Baker & Spice flower as rapidly as it did. I couldn't help but do mental arithmetic, estimating how much my hypothetical 20 per cent would have been worth when the fifth outlet opened, the eighth outlet, the thirteenth... But screw it. Thinking like that would have turned me into a sad, bitter man. What could I do but get on with life? My business might have been stolen from me this time, but I resolved to make sure it would be the last damn time anyone screwed me over like that.

As appalling as I found John Christensen's behaviour over the Baker & Spice affair, this still wasn't enough for him to take top position in the list of total assholes I had to deal with in Shanghai. That prize, by a considerable margin, belongs to a nasty piece of work by the name of Adam Ant (not his real name, but he was a total pest, so let's call him that!), a man who seemed hell-bent on undermining me at every possible turn and making my working life at BakeMark intolerable.

Adam had been sent out to Shanghai by head office four years after I arrived in Shanghai. Business was growing and in his role as general manager he would supposedly provide a wealth of operational and business development experience to professionalise the environment and drive business growth further upward. What a joke that turned out to be. And considering what was to come, it is ironic that I went so far out of my way to help him settle in when he first arrived. I helped him integrate with the staff, invited him to social occasions, and introduced him to some of the most influential people in the city. I was kind at first because I didn't know who I was dealing with.

His true colours came through soon enough. Adam was the quintessential corporate prick, a poet laureate of bureaucratic bullshit and t'ai chi master of shifting blame. No problem was ever his fault and no success was ever anyone's but his.

I've always worked with a great degree of professional integrity. I respected my employer and understood my responsibility to do what was best for the company. The results I was posting for BakeMark spoke for themselves. I might have worked in an independent way and with a certain degree of flexibility, but I knew my accounts and knew how to work them. And I was always transparent with head office. If there was a product problem, I'd explain how it had happened. If distribution was suffering delays, I'd quickly inform them to try and mitigate a customer service nightmare. If I made a mistake, I'd hold my hands up and learn from it. It's always been the way I have been and I knew the big bosses in the head office respected me for it.

To me, this was how business should be done. Flexibly, professionally and as straightforwardly as possible. It is the way I have always been and I know my employers and customers liked and respected me for it. Adam was a different kettle of fish entirely. I think the problem stemmed fundamentally from him being over-promoted and out of his depth. He had no business being sent to Shanghai to accelerate an already successful operation in the first place. He was nothing more than a seasoned pen-pusher adept at snaking his way up the corporate ladder, stabbing whoever he needed to in the back on his way up. When it came to dealing with people, whether colleagues or customers, he didn't have an ounce of common sense.

Under pressure to be seen to be doing something — anything — Adam began muscling in on my established accounts, under the pretence of amping up the account management service but in reality doing nothing more than antagonising and confusing my customers. I started hearing things like, "Dean, who's this Adam fella who just called me about the shipment to Amsterdam being delayed in Singapore? I thought you told me that was all under control?" Or, "Dean, last week we agreed on a 50 per cent discount for this order, why am I getting emails from this Adam Ant telling me the best you can go is 40 per cent?"

His meddling wasn't just annoying, it was damaging my professional integrity and personal credibility. And by doing so, he was making BakeMark look amateurish.

If BakeMark went through a few tough months and the office's revenue figures were below forecast, Adam became even more slippery. Ultimately, the revenue was his KPI, the whole raison d'être for him being sent over with the cushy expat package in the first place. Not that he saw it that way — he didn't hesitate to throw his colleagues, especially if it was me, under the bus if it meant saving his own skin. I saw emails to head office where he claimed Dean had taken his eye off the ball; he was ignoring company policy and giving too much to customers; he was barely in the office and seemed distracted by his extracurricular activities. How could he be at 100 per cent when he's setting up a business on the side and publishing books every five minutes?

This was the most disgusting form of corporate snakery I'd ever seen. It was total bullshit, first and foremost, but also because only weeks earlier we had a chat over coffee about this exact subject. I had explained that I might have other things going on, but not once did I allow any of it to distract me from my primary focus at BakeMark. I might need to break the official nine-to-five schedule every so often and pop out for a few hours on the odd afternoon, but I was in at 5 a.m. every day and usually came back to do an extra few hours from 6 to 9 p.m. And beyond that, well, my phone never stopped ringing from customers in Europe. Adam said, "Oh, you don't need to explain anything to me,

Dean. That's fine. Keep doing what you're doing. I appreciate your work for BakeMark. You do more for the company each morning before most have even turned on their computers."

Funny how he changed his tune when he needed someone else's head to replace his on the chopping block.

Yet that was far from the worst of it. The most shameful episode of all came when, after again meddling in operations he had no part in, Adam fucked up an order and over-ordered hundreds of tonnes of ingredients we didn't need. With no impending orders on the horizon, this was dead stock. All it was good for was the bin, as it would be long expired by the time our customers would be back.

Like I said before, mistakes happen. If it had been me — not that I would ever have been stupid enough to screw up as badly as that — I'd have come clean right away. Resign on principle if I were asked to. Not our Adam, of course. Instead, he sought to cover things up. I might not even have learnt about it myself until I found myself in the warehouse one day and saw an unusual hive of activity. I walked over to see what was going on and I practically had to rub my eyes in cartoon-style disbelief. When I came to my senses, I bellowed "What in the fuck do you think you're doing?!"

I could see what they were doing, but I still had to ask. They were in the process of painstakingly taking the bakery premix (the expired dead stock) and re-bagging it into bags with fresh labels and new — false — expiry dates on them. This was fraud, a criminal act. I felt sick to my stomach. I interrogated the sheepish workers further about who had authorised this. I could only get a few muffled words from the sad bunch: "It was boss. He tell us must re-bag old stock. Nothing wrong, he say." Of course it was.

Working with Adam became a form of daily torture. I could handle myself and I was never truly worried for my job or anything like that. I had just enough trust in head office that they would see what kind of character he was. But the stress came in constantly trying to put out his fires and dealing with the petty nonsense and constant attempts to undermine me. It was exhausting. Thankfully, mercifully, head office finally came to the realisation that they didn't need two highly paid managers in Shanghai after all. Adam or Dean would have to go.

I wonder how comfortable that long flight back to Europe was for Adam with his tail so firmly tucked between his legs.

That period at BakeMark with Adam Ant really formed my hate for the worst excesses of big corporate culture. The sniping, the covering up, the lack of personal responsibility, the passing off of others' achievements as your own. If this was the kind of behaviour that didn't just exist, but seemed to thrive in large decentralised corporate companies, well, it was clear that this wasn't the kind of environment I wanted to work in for much longer. I might have won my war with Adam, but it had left me with a form of workplace PTSD. It was time to polish the CV and pull out my contacts book.

If only business problems were all I had to worry about; this period was one of troubled times on the home front too. After an extended time apart since I first moved to Shanghai in 2003, Susan and Jason finally moved out to live with me in 2006. Susan and I were both determined to give our marriage one more try, for Jason's sake if nothing else. But, in truth, it was never going to work. Something deep down had been broken in our relationship over the course of the previous three years. It was beyond repair.

My behaviour was far from perfect during this time, and there are things I regret terribly, none more so than jumping the gun and embarking on a relationship with someone else before the last rites of my marriage to Susan had been delivered. Our marriage was on shaky grounds for a while because of my relentless pursuit of achieving everything humanly possible, but that was the final straw. Only about a year and a half after moving to Shanghai, Susan decided to leave me and return to New Zealand to complete an accountancy degree she had started. Divorce proceedings commenced almost immediately.

It pained me that what should have been a mutual and mature parting of ways turned much uglier than it needed to be, and I can only apologise for my part in that. All these years later, I am glad that the nastier wounds have healed enough to allow Susan and I to share a great, respectful relationship. I'd go as far as saying Susan is my best friend and I trust her with my life (well almost!). Despite our difficult moments together, we'd never let our problems interfere with us being the best parents we could be to Jason.

It is trite to try and draw positives from such a dark personal time for our family, but, perversely, it did lead to Jason and I bonding in a way we never had before. He was enjoying himself in Shanghai. He had made lots of friends and was thriving in the international school he was enrolled in. So when Susan decided to return to New Zealand, we let Jason choose what he wanted to do. He asked if he could stay with me for another year and finish out his junior school days. He would go back to New Zealand after that for high school. It was a bold move for a 12-year-old, and while Susan was understandably saddened to leave him behind, she respected his choice.

And just like that, I became the primary caregiver in our household, which was quite an adaptation for me. I'd always done my part at home. I'd always been Dad, but I worked such long hours and Susan was such a wonderful mother, that there was definitely a lot of scope for Jason and I to become closer. We had lost time to make up for.

I spoke to head office at BakeMark right away and explained my new personal situation. From now on I could only go to work at 8 a.m. after Jason was safely deposited on the school bus, and I would need to leave at 3.30 p.m. each day to collect him. For overseas trips, they would need to budget a second ticket and hotel room for him to come with me. These changes were accepted, albeit reluctantly. Due in no small part to Adam Ant's false reports, I could sense that BakeMark was beginning to think I was overplaying my hand. At first, though, I thought the flexible arrangements worked fine. Jason certainly did. He loved joining me at big corporate events where he met prime ministers, heads of state, sports stars and TV personalities. I think it was a thrill for him to see me on stage as "Mr Dean", the businessman with all of these important people, while photographers took pictures. Before then he had only ever seen me in the role of home baker and jack of all trades, as Dad.

I particularly recall a business trip to Tokyo I needed to take to meet with a senior executive at Starbucks. While I negotiated a multi-million dollar contract with this guy all afternoon, his wife entertained Jason all over Tokyo. You can see why a 12-year-old chose a year more of this lifestyle before returning to the more sedate surroundings of New Zealand.

Really, having the opportunity to spend more time with Jason was the one silver lining of a very dark cloud. I relished the chats we had every day after school, and our little weekend routine of a morning swim followed by lunch and an ice-cold drink at our condo complex's clubhouse. It's a cliché, but sometimes it really is the simple things in life. Today, Jason and I have a great relationship, and I think we both recognise that our time together in Shanghai was crucial in allowing us to connect as father and son in a deeper way than we ever had before.

The stormy circumstances of the end of my marriage and the fall-outs with Baker & Spice and Adam Ant contributed to a sense of disillusionment and distraction that worsened when my mum was diagnosed with cancer in 2009. All of this combined pressure convinced me that the time was right for a change. Nobody shed any tears when in late 2009 I handed in my resignation letter to BakeMark. They were desperate to find out where I was going, though, and throughout my six-month notice period I was pestered with the question, "Where are you going next? Is it Starbucks?"

The Starbucks thing was a cause of anxiety for head office because they were our biggest client and I had a strong relationship with them. Starbucks (Middle East) and Starbucks (Asia) had in fact made enquiries with me, but neither was particularly attractive. I was 99 per cent sure I wasn't going to join them. Of course, that's not what I told BakeMark.

"Well, I can't go into details but Starbucks is definitely an interesting option for me."

That bought me six months of peace and quiet. Everyone walked on eggshells around me, lest I became their future client from hell. For that half a year I did what I wanted. I only needed to go to the office when anyone from Starbucks was in town.

It was a shame the Shanghai chapter ended on a sour note, because I am proud of the many achievements I made there. In a dynamic and dramatic seven years that included lows as well as highs, I can still reflect on a period of career development, innovative partnership building, the publishing of several more books, and — last but not least — the strengthening of my relationship with my son. When all was accounted for, when I finally left Shanghai in 2010, I did so with few regrets.

My BakeMark days saw me working out of Shanghai, China. So much of where I am today has been developed during my experience there.

At Laris at Three on the Bund, my second home in Shanghai and where I was known as "Mr Dean".

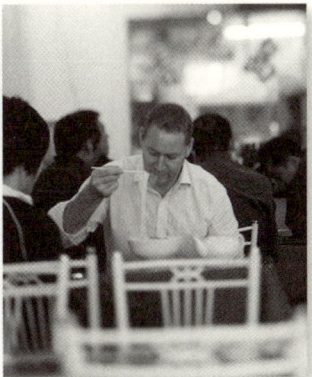

I loved strolling around the streets of Shanghai. Once you get over the glitz and glamour, there is so much to learn.

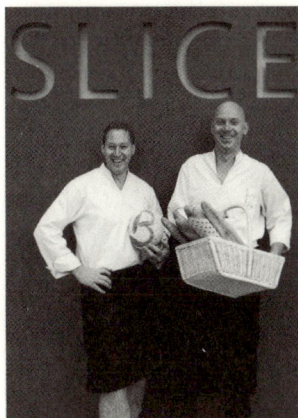

I set up my first micro-bakery with David Laris at SLICE Delicatessen in the Jing Qiao district of Shanghai.

Hard at work at SLICE.

At SLICE, we wrapped a loaf of bread like a gift, using paper and ribbon that had been printed with the 'Global Baker Dean Brettschneider' brand logo.

Baker & Spice, a joint venture by me and the owners of the café chain Wagas, was born in 2008.

The Baker & Spice team in 2010.

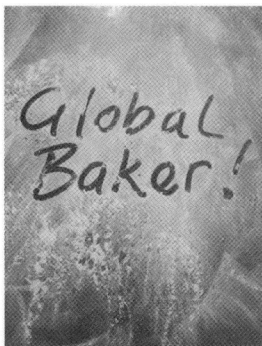

Suffice to say, this was how I felt after setting up Baker & Spice and getting truly shanghaied.

In Shanghai I crafted and cemented my personal brand as 'Global Baker Dean Brettschneider', now retitled 'Dean Brettschneider Global Baker'.

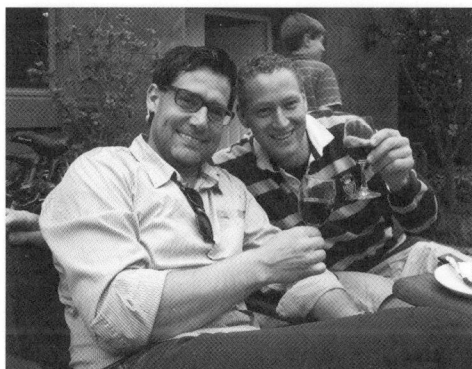

I met Jimmy Carlestam in 2006 and we became thick as thieves. It was his remark on bread in Singapore that led to the founding of Baker & Cook.

Shanghai — as crazy as it sounds — is where I developed my love for cycling.

Seven

Final Rising: Being My Own Boss + Working In TV

I let BakeMark sweat for the full six months of my notice period before finally letting them know a few days before my departure that, actually, I wasn't joining Starbucks after all. I was moving back to Europe to join Lantmannen Unibake. The relief on the BakeMark boss's face was palpable — he knew he had dodged a bullet.

Lantmannen Unibake was another massive corporate conglomerate. Swedish-owned, but with its headquarters in Copenhagen, Denmark, its vast network of companies, partners and subsidiaries were responsible for supplying pre-made baked goods to retailers and eateries all around the globe. If you bought a croissant from Pret a Manger in London or a Danish pastry at a kiosk in an Italian train station, chances were it originated at a Lantmannen Unibake company.

I wasn't joining them as a full-time employee. Fucking hell, I'd have sooner jumped off a bridge than put myself through what I'd been through in the later stages at BakeMark. No, I wasn't going to let myself get stuck behind a desk five days a week at that particular time in my life, not with my side ventures and my need to frequently fly back to New Zealand to see Jason. I was fortunate, then, that the managing director of a company called Bakehouse, one of Lantmannen Unibake's subsidiaries, was an old friend of mine. When he heard I was serving my notice at BakeMark, he got straight on the phone and asked if I'd be interested in coming on board to help him out in a consultancy role. He pretty much let me set my own terms, saying, "Dean, we can be as flexible as you want. Why don't you come in three days a week to help us out where you can? If you need to shift things around to go see your kid, do your books or TV, whatever. It's fine." I couldn't argue with a deal like that.

Bakehouse was based in a large town called Bagshot, located in the south of England, about an hour's train ride from London. Yet, despite my workplace being in the UK, I chose to live in Copenhagen. Yes, Lantmannen Unibake's headquarters were located there, but this had little to do with it. The true reason for my choice of Danish domicile was a personal one, specifically a woman by the name of Vibeke, my future second wife. Vibeke and I had entered into a relationship in the fractious final year of my Shanghai stint, where she too was living at the time. She had left to return to her hometown of Naestved in 2009 after splitting from her husband, and now, in a serendipitous twist of fate, I was moving back to Europe. With an opportunity presented to us like that, it felt natural to rekindle our relationship and move in together in Naestved, which we did in April 2010.

This started a period up until 2014 where I truly lived up to the 'Global Baker' name. From my nominal base in Copenhagen, I travelled here, there and everywhere, burning through passport pages like they were bus tickets. Every Sunday night I was on the night flight from Copenhagen to Heathrow, and from there I had a connecting train to Bagshot for my Monday-to-Wednesday work week, before being back at Heathrow for the return flight to Denmark on Thursday morning. On top of this, there were frequent trips to New Zealand, Australia and various European cities — wherever the wind took me. It was a freewheeling time that helped blow the cobwebs from my mind after the frustrating end to my China days.

The job at Bakehouse was perfect for me. I was on a flexible freelance contract, but I acted more like a full-time consultant. I was working in the innovation and creativity department, something I had become very familiar with by then, but I learnt quickly that the demands of this department were different from what I had experienced in my earlier jobs.

At Goodman Fielder, for example, there was serious pressure on finding frequent solutions to achieve tangible improvement in the manufacturing processes and eventual product yield. At Lantmannen Unibake the atmosphere was more relaxed, with a greater focus on creativity. Because we were working on the end product, such as croissants, rather than base ingredients like flour, the customer experience was at the front of our minds. Our clients were the biggest names in high-street casual dining — Pret a Manger, Caffè Nero, Costa, Tesco, Sainsbury's — and we had a lot of fun pitching wildly inventive product ideas to them.

In truth, the majority of the ideas we pitched, while they were good, never had much chance of being brought to scale. It was all well and good presenting a wonderfully creative and stunningly delicious slice of cheesecake but reality tended to bite when faced with the challenge of producing 50,000 of them on a daily basis for Tesco at $0.06 per unit. Of course, there were still deliverables we had to meet, but only a couple of big ideas needed to stick each year. A couple of recognisable hit products to highlight in Lantmannen Unibake's annual report and the big bosses were happy enough. They just wanted to satisfy the shareholders' demands that the company continued to invest in innovative new product development.

As interesting as the consultancy work was, it was only one element of my life in those days. Fair dues to the boss, he stayed true to his word on the promise of flexibility, enabling me to pursue a number of different projects, including the by now familiar business partnerships and book publishing, but also, for the first time, television work. In fact, one particular venture with a popular café-bakery in Auckland, New Zealand, actually involved all three of these things.

Zarbo Deli and Café wasn't altogether dissimilar to what my vision for Baker & Spice in Shanghai had been, or indeed what Baker & Cook is today. It was a trendy neighbourhood bakery, café and food store, replete with most of the things I associate with that: elegant and minimalist interior design, fantastic quality artisan breads, cakes and bakes, great coffee, excellent service. You get the deal by now.

Zarbo was a trendsetter in many ways, ahead of its time. My relationship with the place went all the way back to when I was working for Goodman Fielder and living in Auckland. I was a regular customer and a friend of the owners, the Chait family. When my first book came out — New Zealand Baker, the one that featured the best bakeries and cafés around New Zealand — I made sure to include Zarbo.

Now, 10 years later, Jason was attending high school in Auckland and I found myself in the city again every so often.

With the success of my Shanghai micro-bakery SLICE fresh in my mind, I got chatting to the Zarbo owners and its resident chef, Mark McDonough, about doing the same thing with them. Terms were quickly hashed out, we installed an oven and, just like that, Dean Brettschneider Artisan Bakery at Zarbo was up and running.

Again, like SLICE, this partnership was more about branding and name-recognition than it was about any (modest) commission that I might make from sales. After being away in Shanghai for a number of years, I recognised the need for some avenues to keep my name in the conversation back in New Zealand, and this was a good opportunity to do that. Of course, this being me, I wasn't going to stop with merely setting up the micro-bakery. During the set-up I said to Mark, "Look, if we're going to be spending so much time together, we might as well do a book at the same time."

Mark, a skilled chef and passionate foodie, didn't take much persuasion. We worked on a concept and structure, developed the recipes and invited my usual photographer Aaron McLean to shoot the photographs for us on location at Zarbo. The end result, when it was published towards the end of 2010, was a brilliant little book whose name might ring a bell with those familiar with the business I am most known for today. It was called *The Cook & the Baker*.

This wasn't actually the first appearance of that phrase. In an earlier book, *The Menu*, which I did with David Laris, there was a jacket flap photograph of the two of us standing below a blackboard with the same phrase written on it in chalk. I'd scribbled it on there while mucking about during the photo shoot and I remember saying at the time, "I really like the sound of that. That's a name for a book or a business name right there."

Mark and I worked well together, and it seemed like the time flew by from the first chat about the book to its eventual publication. Unfortunately, a different publishing project I was working on at roughly the same time suffered a far more storied and laborious production journey.

Before things blew up on the Baker & Spice partnership, in the good old days before John pissed all over our ownership agreement, I had started on a book based on the bakery — its concept, its vision, the recipes and its brand. By the time the break up happened, Aaron had taken all the photographs and the book as a whole was practically complete. Inevitably, the copyright of the book got dragged into the ensuing bitterness of the fallout over the business, leaving another messy dispute to untangle.

Wagas and John kicked up a fuss, arguing that because Baker & Spice was their business and all the photographs had been taken on their bakery's premises, then that meant the content wasn't ours to licence to a publisher — it was theirs. That view, pedantic and small-minded as it was, also happened to be wrong. I had written the text and recipes, and Aaron had shot the photographs, making us the creators of the content. It was simple to us: we owned the copyright.

Aaron really had to fight a battle to get Wagas to release the images. I took a more placatory line as I saw no other choice. With the relationship with the Wagas owners as fractious as it was, I had no desire to fight a long war with them over the rights. Regardless of who was right or wrong on the issue, were it to become a court issue, the book would never see the light of day. My position to John was, "Look, the book's done. The photos have been taken. It's within everyone's interests to publish it. Baker & Spice will get exposure, and Aaron and I get to see our work come to fruition." Mercifully, common sense finally prevailed and *New World Baking: My Time in Shanghai* was finally published in 2011 by a Singapore-based publisher.

By that stage, book publishing was second nature to me; *New World Baking* was my ninth book. Television, on the other hand, was an unconquered frontier. The opportunity to enter into that territory arrived with a phone call I received in mid-2009. The caller introduced herself as a researcher for a New Zealand-based production house, Eyeworks Touchdown. She was wondering if I would be keen on having some discussions about a role on a new reality baking show they were developing. "Of course," I told her, "just let me know what you need me to do".

The conversations, negotiations and screen tests that followed culminated in me being named as the lead judge on *New Zealand's Hottest Home Baker*. I was pleased to get the call, but it wasn't down to luck. Like I said before, I was always conscious about maintaining a profile back in New Zealand even when working overseas, defiantly protecting my 'New Zealand Baker' crown. Evidently, my efforts had borne fruit. The executive producer reaffirmed this when I asked her what led her to contact me, "I don't know, really. Your name was the first one that sprung to mind. And when I Googled the words 'bakers' and 'New Zealand', your name took up the first two pages of hits!"

Principal filming for season one was slated for November 2009, with the show scheduled to premiere across New Zealand in March 2010. I must say, I was excited to be part of it. The format was genuinely original. The concept had been conceived by Julie Christie, the founder of Eyeworks and a reality TV visionary. She was the brain behind many internationally successful shows, including *The Chair, Treasure Island, Trading Places, My House My Castle*, to name a few. After getting to know her personally, I had every faith that *Hottest Home Baker* was set to become the latest of her hits. Today, all the talk is of *The Great British Bake Off*, which has become a global phenomenon, but it is testament to Julie's keen eye for trends that *Hottest Home Baker* hit screens five months before it did. Regardless of what the BBC might claim now, our show was the true trailblazer.

Television work might have been new for me, but I wasn't nervous in the slightest when the first day of shooting came around. I had done screen tests so I had at least been given a crash course on how TV worked — hitting my marks, standing at the correct angles, talking to the camera, all of that kind of thing. It helped that the entire production crew were all helpful, down-to-earth professional Kiwis, headed by Greg Heathcote, the executive producer. Greg directed the production with calm authority while keeping me right on the technical issues and talking me through what he wanted from upcoming scenes. I followed instructions as best I could but struggled when asked to read from a prepared script. It felt so unnatural. After going off script for the fifth time in one particular morning, Greg gave up. "Fine, let's do it your way then. You're undirectable, Dean." I like to think he was only half-joking.

Anyone who has been behind the scenes on a TV production knows that the reality looks very different from what the viewer eventually sees on screen. It was lucky I was aware of this before shooting started because had I arrived expecting any glitz and glamour, I would have been sorely disappointed. We were filming in what was essentially an old garage in an industrial estate. We had to frequently postpone filming when the weather was bad because the rain caused too much noise banging off the tin roof.

This being a brand new show in its first season, the production house did not have a big budget to play with, so a skeleton crew of energetic and hands-on characters shared duties and pitched in wherever they could. Between takes you might have found the cameramen helping to wash the dishes while I brewed the tea, with producers running around blagging (obtaining) props from people's home kitchens. We winged it, basically, and this contributed to a great sense of camaraderie.

The format of the show was pretty much similar to *Masterchef*, but with baking instead of cooking. Amateur bakers competed for the crown of 'New Zealand's Hottest Home Baker', with weekly challenges and bake-offs to eliminate the contestants one by one. I was one of two judges tasked with adjudicating the quality of the bakes and deciding who stayed and who went.

In terms of the tone of the show, Greg and Julie wanted drama. Not overdone, but enough to engage the audience and keep them coming back for more. They wanted a show more in keeping with the high-tension melodrama of American reality TV rather than the more measured style reminiscent of British TV. Knowing my track record as a straight-talking, no-bullshit kind of guy, Greg told me not to hold back on my critiques. "Give it to them straight, Dean. If their cake is shit, don't be afraid to tell them so." But he also taught me the salt-and-sugar approach, in that any time you criticise something, be sure to offer some positive feedback too. You see this from all TV judges; look out for it next time you watch a show. "These muffins are the worst thing I've ever tasted. You totally underdid it with the sugar. But the consistency is good, and the colour is what it should be."

I took to this like a duck to water. Throughout my life I had never hesitated from telling people when they were falling short of standards, so this Simon Cowell role came naturally to me. Don't get me wrong. There was nothing unduly nasty or contrived about my judging. I was always totally fair, honest and impartial in my remarks, and I gave sound technical advice as to how and why they went wrong.

Still, more than a few misshapen loaves ended up in the bin, followed swiftly by the tears of the broken-hearted contestant. Inevitably, this saw me cast as the pantomime villain of the show in the TV reviews, blogs and on social media, particularly so when the contestant reduced to tears happened to be a pretty girl-next-door type, or worse, a sweet-as-pie grandma.

This all made for great TV and, sure enough, when the show aired it quickly became hugely popular among the New Zealand public. A second season was commissioned long before the first season finished its run. In the end, the show went through four seasons, and aside from Greg, Julie and the show's host, I remained the only constant throughout. For each and every new season of the show, there was a different judge alongside me, so I must have been doing something right.

I stayed with *Hottest Home Baker* from day one to the last. The first, and most basic, reason was that I enjoyed the work. Like book publishing, I enjoyed being part of a creative production, learning new things and interacting with a bunch of skilled professionals. Another key reason was that I felt a keen sense of loyalty to Julie and Greg. They took a chance with me on that first season and have stuck by me ever since. Also, unlike the other so-called 'talent' that came and went from one season to the next, moaning about the modest fees and sometimes difficult filming conditions on their way out, I recognised the true value of frequent TV exposure. I was happy not to demand large sums of upfront cash because I knew how to mobilise this publicity to boost my earnings beyond the show. I had my books and businesses, so my prominent TV profile helped drive book sales and create customers.

I knew too that TV wasn't just crucial for sales of existing books, but also for securing deals for future books. If you could tell your would-be publisher that you will be on mainstream TV for half of the following year, a publishing contract would soon follow. TV shows and books have always dovetailed neatly together. The book helps to build the credentials needed to secure a TV gig, while the subsequent TV appearances boost your public profile, which in turn drives sales of your books.

If you manage this cycle carefully, you can generate a wave of publicity momentum that never really stops. By the time the food media has finished reviewing your book, they're calling again to talk about the upcoming season of your show. When that season wraps, oh, what do you know, here's another book off the press ready for review. And on the cycle goes. In this way, during my most prolific TV years of 2010–2014, I published six new books, including two of my most successful, *PIE* and *Bread*, demonstrating the enduring symbiotic relationship of screen and print.

Julie Christie and Greg Heathcote remain close friends to this day, and being influential people in the TV world, they helped open doors to future opportunities for me. Greg, in particular, with his open-minded, can-do attitude, was instrumental. Not long after season one of *Hottest Home Baker* aired in mid-2010, I mentioned to Greg that I was going to be spending a few weeks in Auckland doing the photo shoot for *The Cook & the Baker*, the book I was working on at the time.

In signature Greg style, an idea immediately sprung to his mind. "If you guys are going to be cooking and baking and photographing all the stuff anyway, mate, why don't I send someone over with a video camera and we shoot a behind-the-scenes kind of thing at the same time? We could make a little TV show out of it and stick it on FoodTV." (FoodTV was a cable channel he and Julie co-owned at the time.)

So we did. A videographer came over to Zarbo and joined the book publishing team for a hectic — and cramped — few days. We had to wing it quite a bit for the TV show. There was no real concept or brief, to be honest, but somehow by the end of the shoot, the videographer had cobbled together enough usable video reel for a four-part miniseries, which, like the book, was called *The Cook & the Baker*. Both the book and the show launched in late 2010 and went well, by all accounts.

This same enterprising spirit led to another show soon after. It was called *Kiwi Baker in Shanghai*, shot on the fly at the same time Aaron and I were finishing up the book *New World Baking* in 2011. Despite the ad hoc nature of the production, the end result was a cool show. It was shot gonzo-style with Aaron carrying a cheap handheld camera and following me as I walked around the Shanghai streets, visiting markets, chatting with locals and discussing food traditions and culture. The actual parts featuring me baking were shot later, back in New Zealand.

The concept went over well with viewers, so the Shanghai segment was soon followed by *Kiwi Baker in France* and *A Kiwi Baker in California*. The locations might have been getting grander, but the budgets were not. The shows were made possible only because of crafty opportunism, nifty networking and a belligerent 'why the hell not' attitude that Greg, Aaron and I shared. We persuaded Air New Zealand to come on board and sponsor the flights, so that helped a lot, while a big New Zealand grocery home brand called PAMS injected much-needed sponsorship cash in exchange for product endorsements. When on-location, we stuck to our tried-and-tested production philosophy, which meant basic equipment, bare-bones accommodation and the continuing forced evolution of Aaron from photographer to videographer. In France, I even had the then-teenage Jason come over to act as roadie and help lug our gear around.

Making those shows was a lot of fun, and I was amazed every time I watched the finished shows on TV for the first time and saw how slick they looked after Greg and his colleagues had applied their production magic. Viewers wouldn't have believed the seat-of-our-pants nature in which they'd been filmed. Later, when we did a *The Kiwi Baker (Singapore)* in partnership with the Singaporean media giant Mediacorp, they sent their own team to do the filming, which was quite a contrast to what I was used to. Whereas we'd shot *Kiwi Baker in France* in three days with a crew of two, the Singapore show took two months and an army of staff. I found myself snapping during filming, "I've done this walk-past five times already. Do you really need me to do it again?" Give me the gonzo style any day.

Rick Stein, on hearing of all of this TV work, urged me to get in touch with an influential producer friend of his in the UK called Tim Etchells. "He has some contacts at the Food Network. I am sure he can help set up a meeting." Rick was right. A phone call and a few meetings later, everything was arranged for me to shoot a show in Krakow, Poland. It was to be called *Bake it, Bike it*. The concept was what it sounds like — I was to visit European cities on imagined weekend breaks, cycling the streets, meeting interesting characters and narrating the city's baking culture and heritage. Later, back in the New Zealand studio kitchen, I would recreate the traditional baking recipes I'd learnt. Food Network commissioned it as a one-off short to begin with, but if the audience reaction was as positive as they hoped it would be, then I was in line for a whole series (and beyond).

On the first day of filming, it had been arranged for me to meet the production team of four directly at the London Gatwick airport for our flight to Krakow. I arrived on time but it was only after all the greetings and introductions were over and we were standing in the check-in queue that I realised I had a bit of a problem — I didn't have my passport. After some frantic searching through my bags, the awful truth was confirmed. I must have left it back in my friend's house in central London where I'd stayed the night before. What an idiot. There was no choice but to tell the crew the shameful situation and catch them up on a later flight. I eventually reunited with them in Krakow the following day and filming commenced immediately, albeit a day late. As first impressions go, it wasn't the best.

Despite that hiccup, when filming did get underway, it went smoothly. This being the Food Network, the standards were on a higher plane. Everything was done so efficiently and professionally, using top of the range equipment. Conceptually, the show really worked. Cycling was booming in popularity at the time and what better way to explore a new city than on two wheels? When I saw the final cut of the show for the first time I thought it was a genuinely great piece of television. I was sure it would be a hit.

And it was. Food Network reported that it went out to millions of households in dozens of international territories, and their metrics told them it had been well received everywhere. "That's great," I thought, "but where's my series deal?" It never came. Having deemed the format broadly successful, the Food Network kept it but ditched the Kiwi baker and his bike. The following year, a show called *City Bakes* appeared on screen, hosted by Paul Hollywood of *The Great British Bake Off* fame. Needless to say, the show's synopsis, describing how Hollywood would walk the streets of the world's most evocative cities, discovering the baking heritage of each as he went, rang suspiciously familiar to me.

That annoyed me, but it didn't surprise me. I wasn't naïve. I probably would have done exactly the same thing if I was the commissioner of the Food Network. Like it or lump it, Paul Hollywood and *The Great British Bake Off* were international household names, with 60 million viewers per episode worldwide. And the truth is that the show stood more of a chance with Hollywood instead of me attached to it. That's the fickle nature of fame and the television industry.

The Food Network snub was a mere reminder to a reality that I already had my eyes open to. It hardly came as groundbreaking news that the TV industry was a cold one. I would have needed my head checked if I had harboured any serious thoughts of becoming the next Jamie Oliver or Anthony Bourdain. One reason among many for this is the simple one of geography — New York, London and LA are the epicentres of global showbiz, and I am an awful long way from there. Not many senior UK and

US TV executives are out there painstakingly scouting for talent in Auckland, Naestved or Singapore.

No, international showbiz stardom has never been an objective of mine and I have never let my television work detract from my true focus: my business and my customers. Those are the twin pillars that prop up everything else. Without my successful business and scores of loyal customers, I would never have built the reputation that earned me the invitations to host and judge baking shows in the first place.

I have never lost sight of that, which is why when filming ends for a particular show, I put it straight out of my mind, get my head down and get straight back to the grindstone at Baker & Cook. Back to the daily minutiae of figuring out ways to make my bread taste better, grow the business, widen my customer base and make them happy while I'm at it.

I trust that it is by focusing on these fundamentals that will keep my reputation afloat and my name at the front of producers' and publishers' minds when the next show or book springs to mind. Just as it did when I was asked to host season one of *The Great Kiwi Bake Off*, which is airing now on New Zealand's TV1 as I write this in late 2018. Almost needless to say, a book called *Kiwi Baker at Home* was published almost simultaneously. Season two will follow in 2019.

The cycle keeps spinning.

I moved to Copenhagen to begin my life with Vibeke and also become a consultant for one of Europe's largest bakery companies, Lantmannen Unibake.

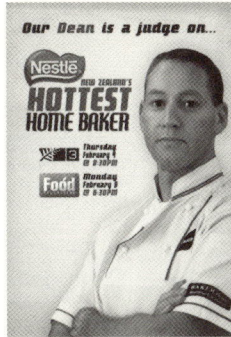

2011. *New Zealand's Hottest Home Baker* was my first stint on TV. There would be many other opportunities following it.

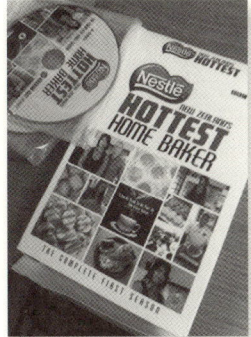

In China I found a pirated copy of the TV series *New Zealand's Hottest Home Baker*. I think only in China would this happen!

2011. Filming *Kiwi Baker in Shanghai*.

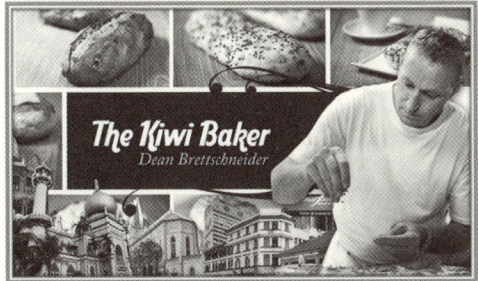

2012. In *The Kiwi Baker (Singapore)*, I checked out various types of local pastries and bakes.

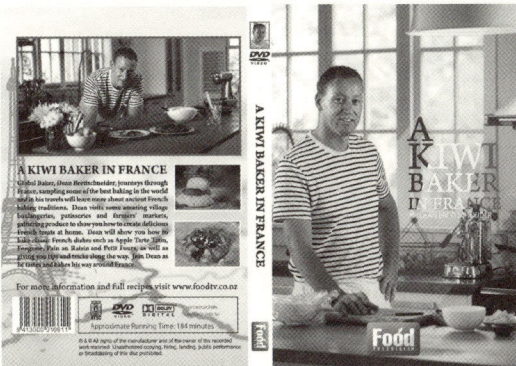

2013. In *A Kiwi Baker in France*, I travelled through France and sampled some of the best baking in the world.

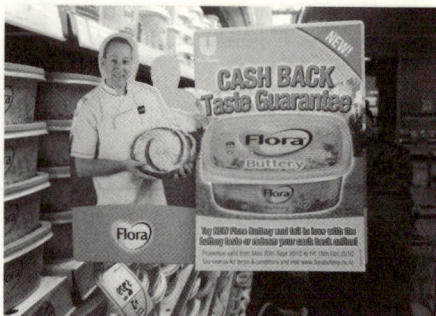
I did my first commercial with Unilever for Flora Buttery.

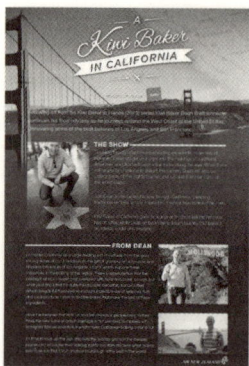
2013. Publicity for the Discovery Channel's *A Kiwi Baker in California*.

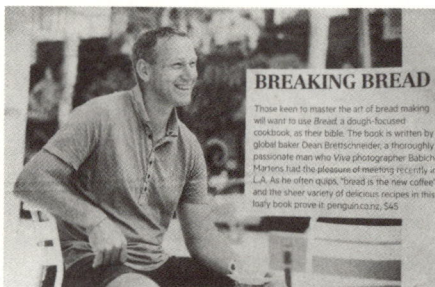
An interview to promote *Bread*, done around the time I was filming in San Francisco.

Season two of *New Zealand's Hottest Home Baker* with Jade Lipton as a judge and co-host Colin Mathura-Jeffree.

The Sugar Club is a spin-off series from *New Zealand's Hottest Home Baker*. It featured Julia Crownshaw (my fellow judge on *Hottest Home Baker*) and I.

2015. Filming in Krakow, Poland with the Food Network Europe on a TV series called *Bake it Bike it*, a people, culture and baking show.

2017. Filming for *Patisserie Fighting*, a Singapore web-drama about baking.

2018. *The Great Kiwi Bake Off* aired in New Zealand. It was a huge success and season two is in the works.

Sue Fleischl, my fellow judge on *The Great Kiwi Bake Off*, and I are flanked by our co-hosts Madeline Sami (left) and Hayley Sproull (right).

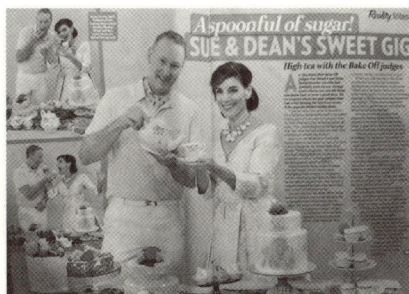

A feature in Woman's Day Magazine on *The Great Kiwi Bake Off* with Sue Fleischl and me.

March 2014. Hanging out with myself at the Dragon Hotel in Hangzhou, China where we created the D'Baker chain of bakeries.

D'Baker opened to great success at the Hangzhou Tower, Hangzhou, China in March 2014.

2014. A poster featuring the IHG Culinary Brand Ambassadors. These chefs are great to work with.

Their Royal Highnesses
The Prince of Wales and The Duchess of Cornwall
request the pleasure of the company of

Mr Dean Brettschneider

at a Reception to mark their forthcoming
Diamond Jubilee Tour of Papua New Guinea,
Australia and New Zealand
at St James's Palace State Apartments
on Wednesday, 24th October 2012

October 2012. My first invite to meet the Prince of Wales and the Duchess of Cornwall.

2015. Another royal invite. I was captured on TV3 in NZ, personally meeting Camilla, the Duchess of Cornwall at a Waitangi Day event in London, UK. It was such a great honour for a Kiwi boy from Waikuku Beach, NZ.

Whenever I'm in Cornwall, UK, I find time to catch up with my good friend Rick Stein and his baking team.

My work with Lantmannen Unibake took me to many places. Here I'm consulting chef Raymond Blanc in London.

April 2014. In the early days of Crosstown Doughnuts. Working on product development with JP Then at Peter Gordon's home in London.

2014. Our first Crosstown Doughnuts store in Leather Lane, London, with Adam Wills at the helm.

2016. Working on new product development for Crosstown Doughnuts with Peter Gordon. We are both founding partners along with JP Then, Adam Wills and Michael McGrath. This is another successful business start-up doing fantastic things in London.

Urban Bakery was a joint venture I owned 10 per cent of, in exchange for developing a range of gourmet supermarket cookies and launching it in association with my brand.

That's a wrap! Filming for Kiwi dairy company Fonterra (owner of Anchor dairy products) took place at Baker & Cook in 2015.

2016. Becoming a Culinary Brand Ambassador to SATS Inflight Catering in Singapore means that my team gets involved in creating bakery products for the airline industry, once again pushing our innovation and boundaries.

كوستا كوفي الكويت تطلق منتجات جديدة على قائمة الطعام

2016. I helped with Costa Coffee Kuwait's food transformation, which was much needed and long overdue.

January 2016. A Kuwaiti newspaper article on my new food range available at Costa Coffee Kuwait.

March 2017. Baking up a storm at Taste Q8 in Kuwait and consulting for Phil Board of Costa Coffee Kuwait.

Eight

Baking: Building A Global Brand

And so we arrive at the tale of Baker & Cook. But to get to the beginning of that story requires jumping back into the midst of those manic 2010-2014 'Global Baker' years. Like my life, this book isn't a simple linear one. Yes, I had my work with Lantmannen Unibake; yes, I was publishing more books than ever before; and yes, my nascent TV career was on the rise. I also had a teenage son in New Zealand to raise and a new wife in Denmark to try and forge a domestic life with. But still a restless drive inside me continued to tick, compelling me to do better — to do more.

Singapore, early 2011. I was there to catch up with a good friend and fellow cycling freak Jimmy Carlestam, whom I'd met during my Shanghai days. I didn't know Singapore well at that point, having only previously passed through on one short business trip. I knew only the basics: Singapore was an economic powerhouse, it was cosmopolitan and English-speaking, and it was hot. Very hot.

I learnt this first-hand when Jimmy took me on an island-wide cycle one early morning during my visit. We were joined by Jimmy's colleague Anders Boye. After a long and sweaty bike ride in 32°C heat, we retreated to Jimmy's place for a cool drink. Talk soon turned to where we should go for breakfast, which had been part of our post-ride routine when in Shanghai. Jimmy and Anders debated between themselves for a few moments before giving up. "Dean," Jimmy said, "there's no good bread in this country. If Singapore needs anything, it's a proper bakery."

Where others might have heard only a throwaway comment, I heard a challenge. Later that day, after a decidedly underwhelming breakfast at an establishment I won't shame here, we took a walk around a sleepy suburban neighbourhood near where Jimmy lived. Called Greenwood, on Hillcrest Road, it was an affluent area, part of the wider Bukit Timah estate, where even the more modest homes go for millions of dollars. Greenwood was a bit rough and ready, but had a charming cluster of shophouse restaurants and bars. One unit stuck out from the rest, a run-down crafts shop at the end of a row of shophouses. A corner site with ample parking out front and a side-street footpath on the long boundary. Love at first sight.

It sounds trite talking about life-changing moments, but that walk around Greenwood truly was. The Baker & Cook journey began with my first glimpse of that dingy corner unit. I knew straight away that this was the ideal site to set up an artisan bakery and food store, which was a point I made passionately to Jimmy and Anders over dinner that evening. Everything I had done in my career up to that point had been priming me for this: the baking knowledge, the networking and relationships, the sales and marketing savvy, my creative eye and the logistical know-how towards setting up businesses. I was ready.

Amid a clinking of wine glasses, the three of us resolved to not let this vision slip by. So while I returned to Denmark and my consulting work, Anders kept tabs on the Greenwood corner unit. After a period of quiet, finally, one day in July, Anders called to tell me the current tenant of the unit was moving out. Did we want to commit to the landlord that we'd take it over?

"Of course, tell him we'll take it," I said.

"You're 100 per cent sure?"

"Yeah, sure, why, is there something wrong?"

"Nothing wrong, except that he wants the $30,000 by the end of today, so we'd better be fucking sure!" he replied.

We weren't going to blink now. Being the man on the spot, it was left to Anders to put down his own money and make the mad dash to sign the Letter of Intent, which was quite the act of faith on his part. Fair play to him. Today, I'm sure he wouldn't admit it, but I bet he had slightly sweaty palms until the wire transfers from Jimmy and I for our share reached his bank account the following day.

That trust shown by Anders backed up what my gut was telling me, that I could take the leap with him and Jimmy. These were good, honest men willing to put their money where their mouths were and back up words with actions — my kind of people. I had been badly burnt with the Baker & Spice situation, but that wasn't going to happen again, not with these guys.

There was much to do before we opened. The first thing was to uncover a bit more cash. Anders, Jimmy and I were all doing okay in our careers, but we weren't driving around in Rolls Royces by any means. I made a few calls around and it didn't take long to attract a fourth investor, a friend called Alex Baumgartner, whom I also knew from my China days.

With the ownership team settled and the cash secured, next came naming our new business. This was the easy part. As I said before, I had long since filed in my mind the phrase scribbled on the blackboard on the jacket photograph of David Laris and me, a phrase that subsequently became the title of the book and TV show I did with Mark McDonough — *The Cook & the Baker*. A simple flipping of that to reflect the fact that I was a baker first and, there you have it: Baker & Cook. Perfect.

Next, I set about nailing down the brand brief. Some might have found it unusual to worry about this before the renovation had even started, but I thought it was crucial that everyone involved in this endeavour knew exactly what Baker & Cook stood for from day one. I won't write the entirety of the brand brief out here, but it included the key ambition "to become the world's leading artisan bakery and food store brand" and that we would achieve this by making "passion our main ingredient". That says it all, really. The bar couldn't have been set higher.

Further to the brand identity, I listed out a number of guidelines and beliefs that I expected all of us shareholders to live and die by, a mission statement of sorts. As well as making commitments to develop our staff, products and service to the highest possible standards, when I look back at it now, two key performance indicators (KPIs) stand out: "build five stores in Singapore within three years," and "open stores across Asia and roll out our brand vision".

As evident, I wasn't going to make things easy for myself or for my partners. It would have been easy to be more modest in our aims — "Make the Hillcrest store one of Singapore's favourite brunch destinations" or some bullshit like that. And we could have done that, no problem. A nice, humble little corner bakery, a steady and loyal business with a return on investment after five years and some pocket money for us shareholders thereafter forever more. Fuck that. Make no mistake, I was entering into this thinking far beyond a single corner store in a quiet Singapore suburb.

Renovations started at Hillcrest Road in October 2011. I had a crystal clear vision of what I wanted for the bakery — an edgy look, sleek and clean, yet with a casual and comfortable vibe that would welcome families and individuals alike. It was a timeless look; it was crucial that the design didn't end up looking dated in two years.

We did our research on architectural firms and ultimately settled on one of the bigger — and more expensive — names. Looking at their credentials and having given them my detailed brief, I expected the design development phase to be a simple and smooth one. How wrong I was. Every step of the process was painful. I literally couldn't believe some of the renderings and proposed floor plans they sent to me. At one stage I thought they had genuinely sent me plans belonging to a different project. "You better tell me you attached the wrong file because what I'm looking at is total shit," I told the guy over the phone.

I ended up designing the place myself. The architect did little more than hold the pencil as I told him what to draw and where on. The firm involved was a waste of time and money, but I suppose it was inevitable I would become so hands-on in designing the place. It was my baby after all, and I was not going to settle for anything less than 100 per cent perfection.

Part of my frustration with the architects was not that they weren't proposing nice-looking interior designs — they were — but that they lost sight of the fact that they were designing a retail space. It's all well and good making a room look pretty, but in a retail environment you can't forget its fundamental purpose. Its entire reason for being is to sell shit.

Designing something that's attractive is easy, but designing something that is attractive and practical is quite another. I understood that better than most, going all the way back to lessons learnt during my Windsor Cakes days. In my design for Baker & Cook, I created a balance of aesthetic beauty allied with retailing practicality.

That very first design, almost without change, has informed every Baker & Cook store that followed. A beautiful bespoke black stone display counter was installed for the baked goods to sit under, which is now our signature look. My display counters were placed right up against the window so that people could see the baked goods from the street. The products were the stars after all. In the store, the most saleable items are placed at eye level, and the less popular items on the lower shelves. Instead of haphazardly displaying the jams and chutneys, they are arranged with contrasting colours next to each other, so each jam stands out and appeals to the customer. Retail 101, perhaps, but I find myself frequently amazed by how many of my competitors can't seem to find the common sense or discipline to follow such basics. I'll take every advantage I can get.

With the design done and floor plans in hand, it was time for the build. Needless to say, that saw its fair share of screw-ups too. Not long after the first hammer was swung, we discovered that in lieu of a proper roof above the baking kitchen, we had a few sheets of corrugated tin over a courtyard. On top of that, a distinctly funky smell alerted us to a leaking sewage pipe running from the second floor down through our shop. Thankfully we discovered it in time or shit literally would have hit the fan.

The additional bill for all this? About $200,000, or $50,000 each per shareholder. It was a very expensive and painful lesson on what can and will go wrong in builds of this type. This had a big impact on how I budgeted future projects. Thankfully, touch wood, we haven't encountered any problems as big as these since, but I always now put in a healthy contingency budget just in case. Since then, we've never had to go over budget and dip back into our own pockets.

Despite the design and structural problems being solved, I started waking up in Copenhagen or London and picking up my phone in trepidation, waiting to see what the latest message of doom contained. There were plenty. One, from Anders, delivered the news that the store just had its windows installed. "But Dean, they're tinted black. You can't even see inside."

When he sent me pictures I saw what he meant. The contractors, in their infinite wisdom, had installed almost solid black tinted windows, the kind you see at sleazy bars and karaoke joints, not once stopping to question if this seemed just a little bit inappropriate for a neighbourhood bakery. The windows were later replaced, but only after a teeth-grindingly frustrating delay.

Next up came a power problem. We were prepared for the need to upgrade the shop's power supply, from 63 amps to 200 amps, to accommodate the huge industrial oven and heavy kitchen equipment that would be coming in. But we weren't prepared for how long it would take. Three months, the authorities told us. So much for Singaporean efficiency. We didn't have any rent-free grace period, so every day spent without power meant another pile of burnt cash. Yet there was nothing we could do but wait.

Finally, on an early January 2012 morning, after the pen-pushers at Singapore Power must have signed and dotted the last piece of paper, we heard digging sounds coming from the road beside the shop. There was a team of workers cutting up the tarmac and laying cables. On a lucky Friday, 13 January, Anders received a text message saying that we had power, all 200 amps of it. After months of waiting, I wasn't going to waste another beat. "That's it, we open on Monday."

Powered by a surge of adrenaline, the head baker and I spent the whole weekend baking our asses off. Those who couldn't bake were put to work on whatever else there was to do, which was a lot. Fixing the displays, arranging the furniture, polishing the floors, calling suppliers, whatever. Admittedly, it was madness to try and ready a bakery for opening with two days of notice but, hell, by this stage such behaviour was becoming our trademark.

On Monday, 16 January 2012, Singapore's first truly artisanal bakery and food store opened. Baker & Cook at Hillcrest Road was a roaring success from day one, from minute one, really. We wanted to become a thriving neighbourhood bakery; somewhere for young professionals to pop by on the way home, somewhere for busy parents to wile away a few hours while their kids slept in strollers beside them, a quiet corner for a granddad to read his newspaper. All the while sustained by quality breads, pastries, desserts and coffee. Judging by the immediate reaction from the public, we had nailed it.

This being a start-up, things were chaotic. Success doesn't come for free. The hours required were brutal. All of our product was made from scratch and both our display and kitchen spaces were modest to say the least, so it required round-the-clock baking to keep up with the demand from the shop floor. And as a new business, there were a thousand everyday matters that become trivial and second nature with time, but at the beginning they create real headaches. Things like remembering the phone number for the vegetable supplier when you suddenly run out of tomatoes at 10 a.m., or trying to recall what the authorities told you about the rules for customer parking. Maybe a staff member doesn't seem to know her arse from her elbow, much less the difference between sourdough and wholemeal, or a kid has just puked on your floor and you realise you don't have a mop and bucket.

I was prepared for all of this. My eyes were open. That's why I routinely worked 36-hour shifts during those first make-or-break six months. It was a gruelling time, but I was up for it. My head baker, David O'Brien, was not. I had personally headhunted him and brought him and his wife over from Shanghai, where he had been working at Baker & Spice. I practically gifted David a 5 per cent stake in the business in return for 'sweat equity' during the early tough months — and he could top that up by buying a further 5 per cent in two years' time at set-up cost. It was a hell of an opportunity to be offered. Sure, there was a long, hard road ahead, but the horizon promised riches.

I was bitterly disappointed, then, when David packed it in after only three months, effectively saying, "I can't hack it, Dean. I'm going back to New Zealand." I did my best to point out that this was always going to be the back-breaking period. It was natural for a new business, but things would only get easier, so he just needed to simply hang on to the tiger's tail and persevere. David didn't listen. A shame, really, none more so than for him. If he had, he'd be a millionaire by now.

Losing our head baker three months in was a damaging, but not critical, blow. Had I not been a baker first and foremost, but merely a businessman investor like the other partners, we probably wouldn't have survived the loss. I stepped into the gap and put in even more hours until we found a new, more reliable head baker to helm the kitchen. Without my expertise of running a bakery on the front line, we would have been sunk.

The head baker wasn't the only casualty. The next to go was Jimmy, after only six months. In June 2012 his company told him they needed to relocate him to Hong Kong. He didn't really have a choice in the matter. To my surprise and disappointment, despite the pending relocation, Jimmy suggested that he should be allowed to keep his shares in the company. I told him firmly that no, that wasn't an option. In our shareholders' agreement Jimmy's shares were predicated on him being on the ground in Singapore, playing an active and genuine role in the running of Baker & Cook. He obviously wouldn't be in a position to do this from Hong Kong. He would need to sell all of his shares.

Regrettably, this led to a temporary breakdown in our friendship and things were frosty between us for quite a long time afterwards. It wasn't easy, but I knew that I had to stay logical and do what was right for the business. On paper, the issue was black and white. That's what the shareholders' agreement was for. Things would have gotten messy if emotions were allowed into it. Truthfully, a compromise probably could have been reached, perhaps if Jimmy had made a more reasonable suggestion, such as holding on to 5 per cent rather than his total 20 per cent, but it is always easy in hindsight.

Jimmy's departure was a real problem. None of us had expected, and definitely not wanted, one of the founding partners to leave after only six months. Aside from the loss on a personal level, there was also the bald fact that us three remaining partners didn't have the money to buy him out. Or at least not without heavily leveraging ourselves with high-interest bank loans. We elected to seek outside investors to plug the gap.

As I just said, it's always easy with hindsight, but how I wish we had just dug deeper into our own pockets and saved ourselves the hell that was to come.

There was no shortage of interest in Jimmy's shares, so we quickly figured that the challenge wouldn't be in finding an investor, but in identifying the right one. We considered offers from an assortment of private equity firms, lawyers, oil tycoons, mall owners and wealthy individuals before settling on a woman whom I'll call Ananya (not her real name).

Ananya boasted an impressive record in the financial industry. She appeared to be sharp, smart and professional; and claimed to be a passionate foodie, ready to roll up her sleeves and get her hands dirty when required. Ananya said she understood that we required her to be a working partner and that we expected her to make contributions beyond her cash injection.

Anders, Alex and I all agreed that Baker & Cook would benefit from her skills and experience in general administration and finance, which were aspects of Baker & Cook that needed greater attention and professionalisation as our business grew. At first, things were promising. Ananya cleaned up and streamlined many of the back-of-house systems, including IT, accounts and human resources; just what we needed. Which is why, initially at least, we could forgive the fact that her confrontational and sometimes bitchy banner was frequently pissing off the partners, staff and even the customers. But even in that 'honeymoon' period, I still had a nagging feeling that this wasn't going to end well.

Before the Ananya situation reached its crescendo, other problems continued to crop up and hamper our growth. After the fun we had with one arm of Singapore's authorities over the power supply, another bureaucratic battle arose over the outdoor seating we had placed in the space outside the shop, an area very popular with our customers. It was a total shock then, when out of the blue, Anders received a call from the Urban Redevelopment Authority (URA) and was told in no uncertain terms that we had to remove all tables and seating at once or risk a massive fine.

Obviously bemused by this, we asked what the hell the problem was. Apparently, as Baker & Cook was registered as a bakery — technically a takeaway business — we were not licensed to provide outdoor service. For months, we tried to work with the authorities to find a compromise, but there was no flexibility at all. The tables went, and with them, $12,000 per week in revenue. This played merry hell with our profit margins. We are lucky we had such loyal and supportive customers, or this rookie mistake on our part could have been a very damaging one. As it was, we recovered from the blow and life moved on.

It had to as things were moving fast. After six months of thriving business at our leafy suburban store, I was keen to strike while the iron was hot and test our model in an urban environment. I didn't think twice when a space became available at 38 Martin Road, a stone's throw from bustling Clarke Quay and surrounded by riverside condominiums. We did the fit-out and opened our second Baker & Cook in November 2012. Like its predecessor, it was an instant hit. Customers streamed through the door from morning to night, and because of its demographic of young professionals with little time to spare, table turnover was much faster than at the more prosaic Hillcrest store. I couldn't have been happier. This outlet was going to be a real money-spinner for us.

And it was, until with more than six months left to run on a two-year sublease, we were given notice to cease business and leave. The primary tenant, the Epicure Group, had decided to close their restaurant and as a subtenant, our only options were to take up the whole space or leave. The space was too big for us so, with great reluctance, we bowed out. Personally, I took this blow quite badly. It had been my initiative to seek out an urban space and target the younger, more dynamic demographic. Seeing the outlet perform even better than my expectations was a source of great pride, so losing it was hard to take.

The opening of our third Baker & Cook at Chip Bee Gardens in Holland Village, in March 2014, helped to soften the blow. The new outlet was located in an absolutely ideal location for us. Holland Village is a well-known enclave of bars and restaurants, with great transport connections. The Chip Bee Gardens side just over the road from there is a bit more upmarket, genteel and surrounded by an affluent housing estate. This gave us the best of both worlds for a customer base — the nearby Chip Bee residents and the spillover Holland Village crowd. We learnt quickly that the customers here were a sophisticated bunch, quite demanding and accustomed to high quality food and service. A hybrid, if you like, between the true neighbourhood folk at Hillcrest Road and the office crowd at Clarke Quay. Today, this modular / kiosk outlet is a star performer in our business.

When I reflect upon this two-year period of business expansion now, it seems all the more remarkable that we managed it at a time Ananya was losing the plot behind the scenes. The thing was, when she simply got her head down and did what she was supposed to do, she did make some useful contributions. Things could have worked out fine had she just kept her mouth shut, did her job, and quietly pocketed her $10,000 per month salary and regular healthy dividends.

Possibly because I was often overseas and Anders was also busy with his day job, Ananya developed an inflated sense of self-importance way beyond her actual status. She would roam around the island from outlet to outlet, walking straight to the back of house to bark instructions and demands to bewildered staff. She would invite favoured friends into the store and have them commandeer both our space and our staff's attention for the whole day, only to comp their meals (provide for free) at the end. For anyone within listening distance, she'd proudly declare how she was the founder of Baker & Cook. My blood boiled when I heard about that claim.

She started to act as if she really did own the place, too, taking unilateral decisions without so much as consulting the other three partners. Sometimes her decisions, while stupid in the extreme, weren't the end of the world. Like the time she decided to replace our elegant glassware with some infantile plastic cups from IKEA.

"These will save us at least $200 per quarter in breakages," she said.

"I'll give you $200 from my pocket right now if it's so important to you, but you're getting rid of those plastic cups tomorrow," I said.

Some of her other attempts at unilateral decisions were not as harmless. I was incensed to hear that she had spent weeks discussing terms with a landlord on a space for a new outlet at a mall called 313 Somerset on Orchard Road, without so much as a whisper to the partners. The first we heard of it was when she called a meeting to sign the Letter of Intent. I told her to forget the meeting and nixed the deal there and then.

Underpinning this impulsive and disrespectful behaviour was Ananya's general ugly attitude; nobody she encountered could stand her. I heard reports of her conniving behind the scenes, playing staff off against each other, reneging on promises. Against this backdrop, Ananya really didn't help her case when she came to the partners demanding a doubling of her already generous salary and a further 10 per cent in shares. Oh, and a personal driver to chauffeur her around. The woman must have been living in cloud cuckoo land.

From the moment she uttered those demands — a crude attempt at blackmail by someone evidently out of her depth — she was on borrowed time at Baker & Cook. Sadly, before we could find a way to get her out the door, her poisonous influence was too much for our minority shareholder, Alex, to bear. He told me and Anders, "Sorry guys, but I can't deal with that crazy bitch any longer. I need to get out."

Alex leaving freed up a 10 per cent stake and the funny thing was, Ananya was licking her lips thinking she would get it. Again, this just exposed her naïvety about business. As per our shareholders' agreement, the 10 per cent would first be absorbed by the company before being shared between the remaining partners on a pro rata basis. Ananya ended up with a mere 2 per cent extra after this, which didn't help her mood.

Somehow, amid this toxic atmosphere, Anders and I had to find a way to drive Baker & Cook forward. There was no way in hell we could trust Ananya to operate things on her own, so we decided to immediately put Alex's remaining shares up for sale. We did so not for the cash, which by then we didn't really need, but to bring in another partner to handle front of house operations. After doing our due diligence and sifting through a long list of interested parties, in September 2014 we decided on a woman with a strong F&B track record, whom I'll call Su-Ann (not her real name).

Hands up here, this was a bad decision. I generally consider myself a pretty good judge of character, but this one totally pulled the wool over my eyes. And talk about adding fuel to the fire. Throwing Su-Ann and Ananya together was like driving an oil tanker into an inferno.

Unsurprisingly, Ananya — embittered that Su-Ann had the shares that she so desperately wanted for herself — went on the warpath from minute one. I recall one crass moment only weeks after Su-Ann had joined and whom at that point had done absolutely nothing wrong. During one of our monthly shareholder video conferences, a minor issue was being discussed and out of nowhere Ananya coldly responded to a seemingly sensible suggestion from Su-Ann by saying, "Why should I listen to your opinion? You do know that everyone at Chip Bee Gardens hates you, right?"

I couldn't believe what I had just heard. It was not only out of context and excessively personal, it was pathetically immature, like something a teenage schoolgirl might say to another. That was just the start. From then on they were constantly at each other's throats, belittling and undermining each other at every turn. The low point arrived at one of our board meetings when the two had a standing, screaming argument in the middle of a busy restaurant. Anders and I cringed with shame as the entire roomful of diners looked on. I'd never seen anything like it.

This kind of shit continued for three more months before I had enough. I called them to a meeting and told them, "That's it, you're both out. If you have anything personal in the office, grab it now, because you will never step foot in any of my businesses again." I explained that they would hear from my lawyer regarding the terms of the buyout and there would never be any future contact directly from Anders or me. A cold and brutal cut-off was the only way.

Ironically, it was only after being booted out from the business that these two nemeses decided to start talking to one another. Again, I can't even begin to understand what was going through their two heads, but they somehow had the impression that my terms were flexible, that if one sold their shares to the other, then the other could swan back into the business. So they got together and started to conspire. Ananya would sell her shares directly to Su-Ann, at a price they arrived at between themselves. Life must be so simple in their deluded heads.

This was ridiculous in two ways. First, I had been clear: both of them were out. For good. Neither would ever set foot in my presence or in one of my stores again. Second, they had no right to discuss and negotiate a direct buyout of the other's shares. They must have thought we had just drawn up the shareholders' agreement for fun, because they clearly had never referred to it. If they had, they would have understood that the business, Baker & Cook, had first option on any and all shares vacated by departing shareholders, and I had already declared our intention to buy Ananya's shares from her. By ignoring this and trying to negotiate with Su-Ann directly, she was in breach of our agreement. Su-Ann, for her part, by agreeing to pay what Ananya had asked for, had fucked up my negotiating position. I could hardly offer less now, could I? Idiots.

If choosing Ananya and Su-Ann as partners in the first place represented two of my worst business decisions, getting rid of them was one of my best. The whole debacle was a frustrating and painful one, but Anders and I learnt valuable lessons that ensured we were more strategic with whom we invited into the operation in the future.

In the end, in early 2015, Ananya's and Su-Ann's shares were sold to Atlantic Partners Limited through Anthony Stiefel, their Asia-based investments director; and Andrew Kwan of Commonwealth Capital, a Singapore-based investment company with a staggering F&B portfolio. In comparison to their predecessors, Andrew and Anthony are like chalk and cheese. Straight away, they each brought creativity, passion and a straight-shooting integrity to the team, as well as bulging Rolodexes of industry contacts and connections. Finally, after two years of boardroom backstabbing, the Baker & Cook ethos had been restored and we were all pulling in the same direction.

Things were well positioned for Baker & Cook in early 2015. The business was strengthened not only by the settling of the shareholders situation, but also by my own personal relocation to Singapore on a full-time basis. In 2014, I had quit my consultancy position with Lantmannen Unibake and moved over from Denmark at a time when the combined pressures of Baker & Cook's growth and the Ananya and Su-Ann fiasco demanded more of my attention than I could provide when 10,000 km away.

With full control of operations at close quarters, backed up by supportive and creative partners, I set about putting Baker & Cook into overdrive. We took up an invitation by the InterContinental Hotel Group to set up a store within its hotel in Bugis, and when we opened in mid-2015, it marked a return to the city centre and righted the wrong of the loss of the Clarke Quay store a couple of years prior.

It was a moment of great satisfaction to see Baker & Cook, which started life as a humble neighbourhood bakery, now standing proudly in a prime city location within one of Asia's most prestigious hotels. I actually think this was a watershed moment for everyone at Baker & Cook. This was our fourth time opening an outlet, but to witness the old magic repeat itself once more, how the customers responded so well to our product, our design, our ethos — it really hit home that we were on to something big. From this, we derived the confidence to roll out stores even more aggressively than we already had been. The proof is in the pudding: as I write, we now have nine outlets in the Baker & Cook empire in Singapore.

While that InterContinental store was being renovated, I was in the midst of pursuing another passion project. I have always loved pizza, and after a particularly outstanding dining experience in a rustic, authentic pizzeria in London, I felt inspired. I decided then and there that I was going to create my own pizza place in Singapore. Not just a branded pizza sold by Baker & Cook, and not just your typical pizza dough. No, I was going to create a new restaurant, a whole new brand, all based around a unique sourdough pizza concept.

Why sourdough? Well, first and foremost, it's different. It's a marketing angle, or what you might call a unique selling point. Nobody had seen the words 'sourdough' and 'pizza' together before. When you hear that term 'sourdough pizza', before you really even understand what that means, it already gives the impression that it can only be a good thing. It's hard to explain, but I think about how people don't just want eggs, they want organic eggs. They don't want to go for just any barbecue, they want to have some Korean barbecue. I was banking on people saying to their friends, "Hey, have you heard about that new sourdough pizza place? Let's go check it out."

And beyond branding, the fact is that sourdough does go hand in hand with pizza. We created a base made using the same fermentation process we use for our famous Baker & Cook sourdough bread. It's made from a combination of flours that are slowly fermented for up to 48 hours at 8°C, using only our natural wild yeast, salt, water and extra virgin olive oil. After pressing it out the traditional way by carefully stretching the dough over our hands, they're topped and blasted at 350°C to 380°C until the crust is super pillowy soft with a touch of crispness. To do the dough justice, I sourced a Valoriani pizza oven directly from Florence, Italy. It is the Rolls Royce of pizza ovens and definitely not cheap or easy to use, but the results speak for themselves.

When it came to naming the place, even I thought it would be going too far to have my name included, well, not explicitly at least. 'Brettschneider' historically meant woodcutter, or carpenter, and this brought the word 'plank' to mind. There you have it: Plank Sourdough Pizza was born. The name had a nice ring to it, and I knew I could play around with the wooden theme in our design identity and materials.

Plank was an exciting challenge from a design perspective because my vision was to have Baker & Cook and Plank Sourdough Pizza physically positioned together, sharing the same kitchen but with their own distinct dining areas and visual identities. The brief, in essence, was a designer's worst nightmare. "It has to look different from Baker & Cook, but at the same time complement it. They should be twins, but not identical twins." Or, as they sometimes say in Singapore, "Same, same — but different."

Yet, as we always do, we pulled it off. The wooden lampshades and dark granite counters at Baker & Cook gave way to a fresh-looking turquoise green feature wall, rough-painted planks in bright colours, and hanging exposed bulbs at Plank. It's like a yin and yang experience walking through the space from one store to the other. Visually separated, if not physically. Both in their own ways are homey, warm and inviting, with large wooden tables for bringing groups together or just sharing, and smaller tables for couples, both indoors and outdoors.

I knew just where to put our first Plank Sourdough Pizza and Baker & Cook combo. Early in 2015 I had signed a lease on a corner site of a row of shophouses, in another sleepy suburban neighbourhood, this time in the lyrically named Swan Lake Avenue in Opera Estate. The site was perfect, located slap bang in the middle of Singapore's picturesque East Coast suburban sprawl, surrounded by condominiums and landed houses. The area was full of young affluent families — and who loves pizza more than children?

We opened in June 2015 and if I'd been the slightest bit nervous about how the thing would fly, those fears were allayed after the first few days. You know you've done good when customers take time to thank their server for coming to their neighbourhood. Evidently, the same kind of neighbourly relationships we'd built at our other suburban stores was transferable anywhere, so long as we stayed true to our methods and standards.

After that, our horizons only expanded. With multiple branch set-ups behind us, a brand new concept launched to great success, and plenty of money in the bank, the question simply became "Where next?" We had 110 per cent confidence in our brands and our ability to identify the perfect locations to capture our tried-and-tested customer demographics. It was just a case of finding the right properties and signing the leasing agreements.

In November 2015 we opened a Baker & Cook in a shophouse in Clementi, on Singapore's west side, followed about six months later by a pop-up kiosk in Holiday Inn Express at Clarke Quay. This store was exciting as it allowed us to give a new twist on our brand, with a limited takeaway-only menu that put us into direct competition with big boys like Starbucks. Bring it on.

Soon after that, in July 2016, we opened our second Plank Sourdough Pizza and Baker & Cook combination store in Bukit Timah, a location I felt we had always belonged to, but for the longest time we couldn't find the right space. When we finally did open there, the wait proved worth it. It rapidly became one of our best-performing stores and remains one of my personal favourites. Towards the end of 2018 we added two more combos in residential neighbourhoods Eng Kong Park and Serangoon Gardens, bringing our running total to nine Baker & Cooks and four Plank Sourdough Pizzas across Singapore. Don't hold me to that number though; we are growing so fast that it will probably be out of date by the time you read this.

With Baker & Cook thrumming along smoothly, the next item on my agenda was to set up a baking school. I had always been passionate about teaching and it made sense from a business perspective. It was just a question of timing. I knew first-hand that the demand was there. Since the Hillcrest store opened in 2012, I would often hold impromptu, informal classes for customers in the bakery kitchen after all the bakers had gone home for the day. But as the business blossomed and the kitchen went 24/7, my bakers kicked me out.

I needed a proper space and I had just the place in mind. There was a hairdressing studio in a corner unit practically a stone's throw away from the Hillcrest store. I even started getting my hair cut there to scout the place out. It was perfect. Finally, after about a year as a secret agent, my hairdresser let slip the intel I was looking for. They were moving out at the end of 2015 when their lease expired. Excellent. Without missing a beat, I got the contact of the landlord and on the following day I signed a long-term lease. With a home secured, planning for Brettschneider's Baking & Cooking School began immediately.

In April 2016, I conducted the very first class, Basic Bread Baking, and practically every class since then has been fully booked, proving correct my instinct that there was a large demand for instructional culinary classes in Singapore. That's not to say we're the only ones doing this sort of thing. The market is actually extremely competitive, but as with Baker & Cook, we always find a way to elevate ourselves above the rest.

For one thing, our teaching programme is the best there is. After all of the experience I've gained in my life and the long list of cookbooks I've published telling people how to bake, I'd be worried if it wasn't. It sounds stupid, but participants appreciate

202 PASSION IS MY MAIN INGREDIENT

the fact that my recipes and instructions actually work. I've lost count of the number of times students have related disappointing experiences from other classes they've tried. And no other school can compete with us in terms of hardware. Our facility was custom-built for baking and cooking classes, inch by inch. Every piece of equipment is of the highest quality possible, imported from all corners of the globe and, as per usual, the interior design is elegant and cutting edge, providing a welcoming environment for our participants.

Yet the school has become so much more than a place to conduct classes. We have noted the pleasing spin-off in how it has become a very effective marketing tool for our other businesses. Every time a class participant walks through the door, we are handed a future loyal Baker & Cook and Plank Sourdough Pizza customer on a plate. What better chance to create a customer than by spending a whole day with them, demonstrating our passion for baking and introducing them to our delicious products first-hand? A student might contribute $100 to our coffers for the class itself, but after enjoying a fantastic course with us, she might make five visits to our stores over the next year, contributing another $100. As her passion for baking grows, she may spend another $100 on my cookbooks to learn more.

It's a marketing cycle, and the school's influence in spreading the Baker & Cook word for us goes some way to explaining why our PR and advertising spend has always been practically nothing. We let our happy customers do the work for us.

If the bakery kitchen across the street from it is the heart of our operation, then the baking school has become the ever-active brain. When it's not being used for teaching, it morphs into our product research and development hub. Many dozens of products on sale at our stores had their genesis on one of the cooking school's bench tops, being tested time and again until perfect. We also use the school for staff training, F&B consultations and corporate events. It's not unusual to see camera crews setting up to shoot corporate baking videos and TV shows. We also bring in guest chefs to conduct specialty classes and have our front-line staff run barista courses.

On the floor above the school is the Baker & Cook head office, where you'll find me plotting my next step towards world domination. There isn't a square inch or spare moment that goes to waste in that building. It truly has become the command centre of our empire.

Nine Baker & Cooks, four Plank Sourdough Pizzas, one Mo & Jo Sourdough Burgers and a Brettschneider's Baking & Cooking School after six years in business — in Singapore alone — is not a bad rate of growth at all. It is odd, then, that every step of our journey has felt organic and sustainable. Whenever a new opportunity cropped up, I felt comfortable and confident to take it on. Not once did I feel stretched or unsure about taking on a new challenge, certainly not from a financial perspective. Everything we've ever done was done with Baker & Cook's own money. We've never had to go cap in hand to a bank, which is almost unheard of for an upstart F&B business like ours.

Of course, as the business grew, the expectations of me as a leader changed. With every new venture came a tsunami of communication, between landlords, construction companies, designers, suppliers, equipment providers and government authorities; and that was just to get us to opening day. Then there's the human resource demands to consider, the management structure to put in place, the ground staff to find and hire. When a new store opens, each quickly develops its own particular set of idiosyncrasies and customer profiles that need to be understood and adapted to.

Needless to say, overseeing the battle on multiple fronts required a different approach to the old days when I had only the Hillcrest store to think about. It would be impossible to keep an eye on everything, everywhere, all of the time. Instead, I learnt, together with my partners, to put more trust in our ever-growing staff, especially our key people. I would never describe myself as hands-off, but I am also far from a micro-manager. If I were the type to stand over my baker's shoulder making sure he was kneading his dough properly, then I wouldn't be able to take on the big picture stuff.

Putting all of the pieces together took time and overcoming plenty of fuck-ups along the way, but we have slowly and surely assembled a management and production team that keeps the whole Baker & Cook train chugging along nicely on a daily basis. This means, for the most part, I can sit in my open-plan office above the baking school, focusing my time on the business's corporate strategy, whether that's a new franchise agreement in the Middle East, a meeting with a real estate agent on a potential new site in Singapore, or sifting through résumés to find a new head chef for the next Plank Sourdough Pizza outlet. All of this, and much more, I do safe in the knowledge that 200 metres away in the central bakery, a highly skilled baking team is pumping out thousands of our delicious products with clockwork precision, ready for delivery to our network of outlets across Singapore.

That central bakery, the heart of everything for us, is a world far removed from the casual glamour of our shopfront that our customers are familiar with. Looking behind the curtain reveals a high-pressure environment where only the bravest and best bakers survive. A bakery production manager oversees a team of 25 bakers, cooks and pastry chefs. As well as the actual baking, he is responsible for ordering the bakery ingredients; looking after quality control, staff management and supplier relationships; and working closely with me on research and product development. This isn't a role for the faint-hearted.

In our bakery, everything is baked from scratch on a daily basis. Everything. We operate 24 hours a day, seven days a week. The daytime bakers are mostly focused on prep, weighing out all the ingredients required for the different types of bread. They also maintain my signature sourdough starter, which has followed me around the world for 30 years. When the night bakers take over, they oversee the mixing, kneading and baking. As each type of bread and pastry is fashioned and finished differently, requiring varying baking times and temperatures, the whole process is a highly coordinated dance, especially as we insist on baking all our breads and pastries just in time. This means we time our bakes to come out of the oven with only minutes to spare before the delivery trucks come to pick them up at 6 a.m., instead of having them ready at 10 p.m. the night before like most other bakeries do.

That is why our stuff is the best. Spare a thought for these bakers next time you are enjoying that warm buttery croissant with your morning coffee.

Today, the gears of our production operation might operate like the finest Swiss watch, but it took time to get here. You tend to encounter some eccentric characters in this line of work. And why wouldn't you? An underpaid, overworked nocturnal job such as baking is sure to attract its fair share of misfits and cast-offs.

In the early years, I received a midnight call from my head baker, telling me to get over to the bakery kitchen as soon as I could. The entire place was a mess — broken eggs everywhere, overturned tables, flour poured all over the floor and counters. We checked the CCTV and watched the screen in disbelief — one of the night bakers had come in at 10 p.m., gone completely nuts and trashed the place before turning on his heel and walking right back out the door. We never saw or heard from him again. Who knows what set the crazy bastard off? He must have had some serious issues.

As for the post of head baker, well, we might as well have an installed a revolving door in the office for that. We went through four in our first four years. You know about David O'Brien's disappointing cameo already, and his successor didn't last much longer. The third man to take on the hot seat, another Kiwi, turned out to be a raging alcoholic fond of sleeping off his hangovers in the early morning hours on the floor of the bakery kitchen. Again, this was something I discovered by looking back on the CCTV footage, which was proving more dramatic than anything I saw on my TV cable channel at home.

As soon as the whiskey fumes from the third guy had dissipated, we brought in his replacement, hoping to be fourth time lucky. Number four was a young Aussie baker, who arrived with an impressive résumé and decorated with many awards. He was as arrogant as he was enthusiastic, ready to take on the world without anyone's help or advice, least of all mine. After a patchy year in the job, he decided to redefine his own role, becoming the world's first non-baking head baker. But before he could get himself the sack for that, he chose instead to earn his marching orders by starting a fight with another staff member. I have no idea where this young ass ended up, but with an attitude like his I seriously doubt it's anywhere good.

Unfortunately, issues with staff continue to crop up with irritating frequency. Over the years I have learnt that regardless of how much homework you put in during the recruitment stage, or how meticulous you make the training process, some people will still let you down. It's a sad fact of nature — no matter what you do, some people are just irresponsible, ungrateful and selfish assholes.

Two cases spring to mind straight away – not hard, really, given that they both happened in the past month while working on this book. The first one was a pretty senior guy in one of our most popular stores. He had worked with us for a couple of years and was a well-liked member of the team among his colleagues. From what I had seen of him, he seemed alright at his job. No problems there. That was until it came to our attention that the outlet's accounts had started to show an unexplained decline in takings for several weeks in a row. We delved into it further and spotted an unusually high number of voided receipts. It didn't take Sherlock Holmes to find out what was going on.

A quick check of the security footage told us what we needed to know. A couple of times per shift, long after the customers had paid for their meals and left, this guy was voiding their receipts and pocketing the cash from the till. Each receipt would easily have been in the $50 range, so doing that twice per shift over a long period of time — we checked to confirm he had been doing it for two months at least — meant that the slimy bastard had taken thousands of dollars from the company.

Case number two followed soon after at a different outlet. Another thief, but a different method. This lady, a store manager, was doctoring vendor invoices to make it look like we were being charged more than we were for maintenance services and such. The smoking gun we caught her on was a plumber who came to fix a leaky faucet. He charged $100, wrote up the invoice and passed it to her for payment. The store manager, as per our practice, paid him from a petty cash float we have at each of our outlets. The crime came later when she took a ballpoint pen and changed the $100 to $200 on the docket and took out an extra $100 from the cash float for herself.

In both cases I was staggered by the gall shown from the two thieves, not to mention their stupidity. Did they really think they wouldn't get caught? As soon as both events came to light, I had no hesitation on how to proceed. First, they were sacked, immediately and without debate. Second, I called the police. The latter decision naturally took more thought than the first, but I didn't labour over it. For me, behaviour such as this went beyond business; here, basic ethical codes had been broken and lines crossed.

As these unsavoury incidents played out, tears were shed and recriminations made. Their friends and colleagues pleaded on their behalf and I wasn't Mr Popular among the staff when they were being led away in handcuffs. That's not nice to see, but there were no regrets from me. This is the price you pay when you betray both your employer's faith and break the laws of the land. I try my best not to take such actions personally, but it's not easy when it's your name on the door, when the business is your baby and your pride and joy. As far as I'm concerned, having a staff member steal from Baker & Cook is little different to a family member stealing from my own home. It leaves a very bitter taste in the mouth.

Morality aside, it is important to set a precedent when things like this happen. Had I let them off, how would that make me look to the other staff? I'm sure it wouldn't have taken long for them to share their methods and explain how easy it was to get away with it. Before I'd know it, half of my staff would be doing the same thing. In fact, I have no doubt that some other staff members probably have sticky fingers too — probably not to the same extent as in these two cases, but it's harder to keep track of bread and pastry pilferage and the like. Perhaps the memory of the police cars pulling up outside our store will make them think twice next time.

Thankfully, the revolving door of head bakers and the recent events with the two thieves represent rare lows of Baker & Cook personnel. The majority of our staff know that they will not get far in the F&B business unless they are willing to put in the hours and get their hands dirty. You can have an ego the size of Donald Trump's for all I care, but you better damn well understand that ours is a tough, messy and thankless business for the main part, and there will be times when all hands to the pump are needed, job titles be damned.

It comes down to attitude really, and there are a couple of occasions that spring to mind when I think about what I want to see in a member of staff.

On an Easter Sunday a few years ago, the Hillcrest store was expecting a roaring trade on our hot cross buns, which had flown through the door in previous years. We'd already racked up huge back orders this time round but when I checked in that morning,

I saw that the baker had ballsed up the recipe — they came out of the oven looking like shit. The store manager cringed when she saw them and immediately said, "We can't sell those," and tossed the whole lot in the bin. She didn't so much as look in my direction for affirmation. I liked that — no fudging the issue, no bullshit. In plenty of bakeries elsewhere the staff member might even have shrugged and tried to sell them anyway. At Baker & Cook, we don't waste time on recriminations and moaning. Mistakes can happen. We just got down to replacing the buns, rolling up our sleeves and baking like our lives depended on it. At 3 p.m., the buns came out perfectly, a few hours late, sure, but we delivered.

Another day, this time at Chip Bee Gardens, the chef didn't show up. If that happened anywhere else, the branch manager would have simply scrawled a message on the chalkboard saying that the cooked food items on the menu were unavailable that day, sorry. But not at Baker & Cook. Instead, without any prompting from me, the manager grabbed the recipe manual and a whisk and started scrambling the eggs herself. Initiative, guts, commitment. Beautiful.

That attitude is what we are all about. Our commitment to the highest quality customer service is non-negotiable. When I first arrived in Singapore, I quickly noticed that service standards in F&B were terrible, and the reason was quite easy to identify. Nobody had any respect for service roles, regarding them as low-status and low-value jobs. This disrespect naturally led to apathy and laziness among staff. If they were being disrespected by customers and paid peanuts by their boss, why should they give a shit? We do things differently at Baker & Cook. Our people are paid and treated like the professionals they are and high standards are demanded of them. This is the way it should be and, ultimately, everyone benefits. The customers receive a high level of service and our staff can go home proud of a hard day's work.

In 2016, we knew the time was right to challenge our business beyond Singapore's shores. I had not forgotten that one of our mission goals was "to become the world's leading artisan bakery and food store brand". Note that I said the world, not just Singapore. We had the utmost confidence in our formula and brand by this point. The fact we had made it work in Singapore's ultra competitive and demanding market was no mean feat, something that gave us gravitas and respect among the many potential foreign partners we had discussions with. We received enquiries from a number of neighbouring South East Asian countries, the Middle East, Japan, India, even the USA, and I met with all of them. It was just a matter of finding the right fit for us.

Of the many possible locations presented before us, it was Manila, Philippines, that kept circling in my mind. I knew the city reasonably well, having done business there in the past, including consultation on the setting up of the gourmet food brand Dean & DeLuca. Manila was home to countless international companies, with a heavy USA-leaning influence, and it was evident that to many young, aspirational Filipinos, foreign companies came with a stamp of quality and an Instagrammable cachet that local businesses didn't have. In a country where appearance counts for a lot and social media is king, I knew that Baker & Cook's profile and aesthetics could make a serious dent in the F&B market.

With the choice of city sorted, next up was finding the ideal partner. Step forward, The Bistro Group, Philippines. Having first been introduced via a government agency that facilitated international business connections, we soon set about selling ourselves to each other. I did my homework on The Bistro Group and liked what I saw. Similarly, their chairman, Bill Shelton, was drawn to our vibe, products and design. Once he understood the Baker & Cook and Plank Sourdough Pizza model of combining the two brands side by side, sharing the same kitchen and service staff, making money in the morning with the bakery until late at night with the pizza joint, he was hooked.

After a good phone conversation, Bill immediately arranged for a delegation to come over to Singapore two days later to check out our operation on the ground. A day after that, the memorandum of understanding to franchise a Baker & Cook and Plank Sourdough Pizza in Manila had been signed. Clearly, just as I am, The Bistro Group was all about getting shit done. I was impressed.

A site was chosen in the upmarket S Maison Mall, the swankiest part of the Mall of Asia complex on the shore of Manila Bay. The construction and fit-out was done according to my specifications, and all the elements of our signature look fitted well into the space, including the non-negotiable Valoriani pizza oven. In terms of staffing, I knew I didn't have to worry. Filipinos are passionate people and customer service is taken very seriously, so I was convinced that our high Baker & Cook standards would be met by the team there.

We had read the runes correctly. Manila was ready for something different and queues of people formed on the morning of the official opening of Baker & Cook and Plank Sourdough Pizza in the Mall of Asia on 11 January 2017. Six months later, a second Baker & Cook outlet opened in June 2017, in Quezon City.

It was a proud achievement to see the Baker & Cook name bear addresses in a different country. After all, it had only been five years since we were waiting anxiously for Singapore Power to give us the amps we needed to open up our first shop on Hillcrest Road. Our little bakery was all grown up. But opening a place overseas is one thing. Making a success of it is another. Yet much like all the outlets we had previously opened in Singapore, I didn't have a shred of doubt about Baker & Cook performing well overseas.

The fact that the franchises have performed so well in Manila is a credit to the fundamental strengths of our products, visual identity and brand values. But we were also very canny with our marketing of Baker & Cook in the Philippines, especially prior to its launch. The Bistro Group and I fully understood that to gain international traction we would need to double down on my personal name and brand. Having a celebrity TV baker spearheading the company was critically important, as my profile was the only thing we had to mark us out as different from the thousands of other cafés and bakeries fighting for customers' dollars. We pushed my name and credentials heavily in the pre-opening PR push, and, at one point there was even a 30-foot billboard of my face adorning the outer wall of the entire mall. Having been accused of being big-headed for most of my career, this was a literal new twist on the term.

Judging by the queues on opening day and our success since, our efforts in Manila worked. From then on, it would have been tempting to target rapid expansion, to barrel ahead at 100 miles per hour. That would have been a road to ruin. Overseas growth demands a careful and considered approach. The logistical challenges, financial implications, cultural sensitivities and language issues are all factors to think about, challenges on a totally different scale to what I worry about on our home turf in Singapore.

With this judicious approach in mind, after the Manila franchise was up and running smoothly, I could turn my attention to getting a slow-burning opportunity off the ground. Saudi Arabia had been on my horizon for several years, since the setting up of Baker & Cook outlets at the InterContinental Hotel and Holiday Inn Express in 2015 and 2016 respectively. The ultimate brand owner of those two hotels was the InterContinental Hotel Group (IHG), for which I also acted as a global brand ambassador. Over the years, we shared several conversations on how I might be able to bring Baker & Cook to their home turf in the Middle East.

The first tangible step came in late 2015, when IHG invited me over to Al Khobar, a city right on the eastern coast of Saudi Arabia and a stone's throw from Bahrain. They had an InterContinental Hotel there with a recently vacated, street-facing space that they thought would make an ideal Baker & Cook.

I happily took them up on their invitation and flew over there at the first opportunity, all expenses paid, and soon came to the conclusion they had arrived at — this would work very nicely indeed. The city was affluent, the area heavily populated with families, and the unit space was nicely situated and proportioned. All I needed to ask was, "Where do we sign?"

I was soon to learn that business in the Middle East didn't move quite at the pace I was used to. This was merely the first step in a four-year-long courtship — a big difference from the norm in Singapore, where I usually get angsty if we're not up and running after four months.

Of course, there are complex issues at play in an overseas franchise deal like this one that require patience and diligence. Manila is different from Singapore in many ways, but food tastes and customer profiles were at least still on the same wavelength. These things were different in the Middle East and more time needed to be spent on localising the Baker & Cook package. It was interesting for me to work with the franchise partners on developing the menu for the local palate and expectations. For example, things like tzatziki, hummus, flatbreads and baba ghanoush will all appear on our menus over there.

Still, I would have preferred the deal to have been wrapped up quicker than it did, but the truth is, there was little I could do about it. In franchise deals like this, it is the franchisee who calls the shots. It is their money and their risk after all, so you have to play by their schedule.

The working style of that courtship period was quite an eye-opener for me. We might exchange a couple of emails in December but then there would be total radio silence for six months. Totally out of the blue, my phone would then ring from an unknown number and the voice on the other end would say, "Mr Dean, the Sheikh will be in Bahrain next Thursday. It is my pleasure to invite you to have dinner with him and his team of advisers. Please confirm you will be available and we will make the necessary preparations for you."

"Yes," I'd say, "of course I'll be happy to accept this invitation," being pretty sure that saying no wasn't really an option. With that, an email would soon follow with flight details and a brief agenda of what the Sheikh wanted to discuss. Come the following Thursday, upon arrival in Bahrain, I'd be picked up by a waiting car at the airport, driven straight to the hotel and shepherded to my seat in the hotel restaurant. I'd have a nice meal and discussion with the Sheikh and his team for a few hours before the goodbyes were said and I was driven back to the airport for a midnight flight back to Singapore. And the following morning I'd think to myself, "Did any of that actually happen?"

Glacial pace or not, it all proved worth it when we opened our first Middle Eastern Baker & Cook outlet at InterContinental Al Khobar, Saudi Arabia, in mid-April 2019. A Baker & Cook and Plank combination outlet followed in a nearby luxury mall the month after. Not that these launches went without hiccups. The latter outlet faced a month's delay when, a matter of weeks before opening, the Sheikh visited the two-floor space and casually remarked, "I think I'd like to have a lift here. I don't think our customers will want to climb so many stairs."

Last minute issues aside, I was very proud to witness the opening of these two flagship Middle Eastern outlets. The further from home base you see your business take life, the more of an achievement it feels like. I can't help but think that I really have struck upon something special when I stop to think about the fact that, today, someone ate and enjoyed my bread in Saudi Arabia, in the Philippines and in Singapore. Soon, I'll be able to add the United Arab Emirates to that list, having just signed off on the master franchise deal for that territory. We are in the midst of looking for suitable sites now.

The Manila, Saudi Arabia and United Arab Emirates partnerships are all franchise deals. For many companies seeking a presence in unfamiliar overseas territories, it is the easiest and quickest way to enter a market. The way it typically works is that the franchisee pays you a nice upfront sum and a royalty of future revenue — for argument's sake, let's say the upfront sum might be US$200,000 and the royalty 5.5 per cent. For that, the franchisee gets the rights to use your brand name, and you provide them with the secrets to your success: a franchise manual containing your recipes, your design identity and guidelines, statistics and customer profiles, and various other things that advise them on the DNA of your business.

After that, the entirety of the financial risk is on the franchisee. Construction, renovation and equipment costs, marketing and advertising, staff training — even further consultation from me costs extra — is all on the franchisee. Depending on the nature of the franchise agreement, materials like branded packaging and associated collaterals such as stationery might also be an additional cost.

In this sense, many regard franchising as a risk-free enterprise for the franchisor. "It's so easy. You don't spend a cent of your own money, but you'll bank a nice upfront sum and wait for a new business to sprout up overseas? You have nothing to lose!" While this is fundamentally true in a simplistic sense, that's not how I see it.

First, I don't consider entrusting my baby to a relative stranger to be risk-free, regardless of how much I get paid to do so. What if they fuck it up and damage my business's brand and personal reputation? When I sign off on a franchise deal, I am committing to the partnership wholly. Taking a back seat and watching as a franchisee makes a mockery of everything Baker & Cook and I stand for would never be an option for me. A mere US$200,000 would be no consolation to watching a Baker & Cook franchise go under. My business and personal integrity will always be worth more than any sum of cash.

You also have to spin the question around: is it not a risk to give away the formula of your business success for a modest sum of cash and future royalty? I think it is. As a franchisor, you naturally want your franchises to perform well, but not too well. If I received a $1 million royalty payment from a franchisee for the previous financial year quarter, it won't take long for my initial happiness to turn to, "Fuck, if my 5.5 per cent is worth this much, those bastards must be killing it." You don't want to become the guy who sold McDonalds for a dime.

There is also the opportunity cost. Setting up an overseas franchise — if you want to do it responsibly, that is — takes a lot of time and effort. Time and effort that could be spent making money for your business elsewhere. Does that US$200,000 lump sum look so attractive when you think of the hundreds of hours I and my staff poured into making a particular franchise deal happen? What if all those flights and business trips — all that time spent consulting with and helping a franchisee and developing new recipes for their menu — inadvertently cause standards and revenue to slip back home?

No, there's no such thing as being risk-free in business. Franchising is a legitimate and attractive partnership option, but it takes very careful consideration. Picking the right partner is absolutely crucial. A massive amount of respect and trust is needed from both sides.

For me, I need to be convinced that a franchise partner truly understands everything about me and my business. And I mean everything. That extends from my own personal story to my baking techniques, to Baker & Cook's mottoes, ethos, brand identity — the whole shebang. They also need to persuade me that they will execute their business plan effectively and represent my good name appropriately. On the other side of the coin, a franchisee needs to be convinced that their country truly needs my product and brand. Why is my bread so special? And once they're convinced on that score, they need to know that I will be there to support them through the journey, and that I will be open and flexible enough to trust their advice on how best to adapt and localise my offerings to their customers and culture.

Genuine relationships are at the core of all strong business partnerships and I am pleased to have formed such good ones with my partners in the Philippines and the Middle East. Because of this, I can confidently look forward to seeing the overseas Baker & Cook franchises thrive for years to come.

Ironically, while we hit it out of the park in the Philippines and Saudi Arabia, countries both geographically and culturally distant from Singapore, it has been our closest neighbour, Malaysia, that has caused us the biggest headaches in our overseas efforts. This, to be clear, should not be the case. Malaysia, a mere hop, skip and a jump over the Causeway from Singapore, should have been a simple home run for Baker & Cook. Even now I bristle with irritation to think that we haven't got up and running there yet. It hasn't been for a lack of effort and commitment on our part — far from it.

It was 2017 when we first entered into serious discussions with a huge Malaysian investment holdings company (that's listed on the country's stock exchange). By February 2018, we had agreed to the terms for a joint venture agreement. The company is an influential player in Malaysia, with significant holdings in retailing, hotels, property development, confectionery and much more. Their knowledge of how to set up and conduct a business north of the Causeway would be a major boon for us. So far, so good.

This partnership was to be different from the franchise deals we had done in the Philippines and the Middle East. Other than franchising, there are two other ways to do business overseas. You can either set up the business on your own, using your own capital and taking all the risk on your own shoulders, as we had in Singapore with Baker & Cook in 2012, or you work with a partner on a joint venture (JV). You share the start-up costs, liability and – eventually, hopefully – the profits.

Setting it up ourselves wasn't a realistic or attractive option for us. Malaysia might only be an hour's drive from my office at Hillcrest Road, but the country's business regulations, employment laws, commercial property rules, supply chains and everything else that goes into setting up a new F&B business were unknown to us. We could have learnt, sure, but it would have taken an army of lawyers, far too much time and a boatload of cash just to get to the start line. We had to ask ourselves if we really had the appetite for all that. We didn't.

A joint venture made sense, then, especially with a partner of this size and credibility. We could let them exercise their know-how in their home country and navigate the legal and bureaucratic minefields for us. On top of that, with so many attractive property holdings, there was no doubt they could find a good space for us to set up shop. The terms of the deal were classically simple too: 50-50. We committed to putting in $250,000 each to get started and, later, profits would be split down the middle too. Things couldn't have been clearer.

When we signed the deal in February 2018, the outline of the plan was for a Baker & Cook and Plank combo to open in one of Malaysia's best known department stores, as part of Mid Valley Megamall in the heart of Kuala Lumpur. This particular department store, owned by our JV partners, would be going through a complete renovation from head to toe to turn it into a trendy lifestyle store. A Baker & Cook and Plank combo, together with a Brettschneider Baking School, would become a key tenant on its F&B floor. We slated the opening for October or, at the latest, November 2018, which gave us a comfortable timeline.

I did have reservations about the proposed space. Malls had never been a natural home for our suburban vibe. I really wanted to go into the neighbourhoods and simply repeat the formula that had been so successful in Singapore. But our JV partners put up a good argument and reassured me somewhat. Their new lifestyle concept would vacuum up the aspirational millennial crowd, the type of coffee culture kids who would flock to Baker & Cook. This, in fairness, was a similar idea to what had proven successful in the Manila franchises. Okay, let's do it.

Initially, progress was smooth. The joint venture company was duly registered, and floor plans were swiftly drawn up, amended and approved. We were so comfortable with how things were proceeding that we even went ahead to buy much of the equipment we needed. In July 2018, I hired an excellent new general manager (GM) to handle the final few months of pre-opening work, and in September I hired eight new staff members. As far as I was concerned, everything was on track for opening in October as planned, or, if absolutely necessary, November.

Perhaps I should have paid more attention to some alarm bells as the year progressed. There had been irritating, unexplainable gaps in communication with our JV partners from time to time. Simple yes-or-no questions were often left hanging in email threads, or scanned documents I asked to see were conveniently missing from the email replies. But at the time they weren't the sort of things causing me to lose any sleep. I trusted that my partners were doing their part to stick to our agreement and timetable.

I became more concerned once my new GM was on board and on the ground in KL. Her reports of the department store that had not begun any construction while we were four months from our proposed opening date wasn't much cause for comfort. Nor were the debriefs of her meetings with the JV partners' project team, where they seemed bizarrely shaky on basic operational details, such as whether or not the electricity permit had been applied for yet. In such cases I would follow up in search of answers. All through June, July and August, every time I asked how things were going, "Fine, Dean; all is on track," was what I was told.

I might call to check on the extractor fans I knew had been delivered the day before, asking if they have been installed without a hitch.

"Yes, Dean, they put them in with no trouble at all."

"So how is it that I am looking at pictures of the fans still in their boxes that my GM sent me literally just five minutes ago?"

I was unnerved, naturally, but I pushed ahead. In September I brought the new staff (finance personnel, front-of-house manager, and six bakers and pastry chefs) to Singapore for a month of intense training. When that was done, I called my JV partners to tell them that we were ready to rock and roll. They just needed to confirm when the department store was reopening so that we could plan our launch party. From here, the web of deceit unravelled.

For the first time in months, they told me the truth. There would be no opening in October. In fact, there would be no opening this year. The most optimistic projection now, I was told, was April 2019. They went on to say that the new lifestyle part of the mall had barely begun renovations, many of the spaces still had no tenants and, oh, by the way, the space they had marked out for us needed to be changed. There had been some misjudgements; our floor space was infringing too far into the general mall space and they would need to revise the floor plan to adjust the boundary line.

I didn't know whether to laugh or cry. There I was with equipment waiting to be plugged in and a team of enthusiastic, fully trained staff and now they were talking about going back six months in the process to relook at floor plans. Make no mistake, this situation was beyond one of mere irritation; this was a total shit show. We had already burnt through half of our start-up capital — $125,000 each — on set-up costs, equipment, training and staff, and now they were telling me I had to wait another six months to open? What the fuck was I going to do with eight staff members in the meantime?

The situation was untenable. In one of the most difficult decisions of my professional life, I had to let go of the new staff we had hired and trained but who never actually had the chance to work for us. We simply didn't have the funds available to retain them for an indeterminate amount of time without work being done and revenue coming in. The only silver lining was that I at least managed to retain the GM and folded her into my Singapore operation.

Bristling from the personal embarrassment and pain from letting all of these would-be new staff down, I called up my counterpart within the JV partner company to tell him I was done. I was pulling the plug on the project. I said to him, "I still have faith in Malaysia and I still have faith in you [the holding company], but I have zero faith in your department store and will never work with them again."

My JV partner was surprised to hear just what a balls up the department store's team had made of things. He tried to talk me down a bit. "Don't be hasty, Dean. Can't we do some pop-up stores or something while we wait for the store to be renovated?" No chance. I wasn't going to be messed about with any longer.

The JV partners knew there wasn't much they could do in the matter. The department store was their company and the proof of their incompetency was there for all to see. They weren't happy about how things had played out either — their money had been pissed up against the wall just as mine had been. But in the end, they had no choice but to agree to my demand to freeze the joint venture and its bank balance for the time being. Nothing was being dissolved, but we would just leave things on ice and when the time was right, we could take things back up and try again. But next time, we'll do things my way. My Malaysian friends, we'll be coming to a neighbourhood near you soon.

Valuable lessons were learnt from the failed project. With some time to reflect, I see now that a fundamental problem was that our partnership had been made with the people at the holding company, people we liked and trusted. But once the paperwork had been signed, we were left dealing with their department store team, a bunch of retailers who were clearly out of their depth working on an F&B venture. The fact that right up to the end we were dealing with mid-level executives — who had job titles like

'Retail Marketing Manager' — says a lot really. The people we ended up working with just didn't know our business. In future, I will make sure I know precisely who we will be dealing with on a day-to-day level before any partnership agreement is signed.

I also know now that I should have stuck with my instincts in the first place. It is not just that the mall environment doesn't really suit us, it's that the working structures and processes that are involved in a mall environment don't really suit us either. Give me my leafy neighbourhood corner unit, a hands-off landlord and let us get on with it.

And not that I needed any reminding, but nobody said business was supposed to be easy. We are spoilt in some ways by how efficient Singapore is. Similarly, the Bistro Group were such perfect partners in Manila that our franchises were set up with me barely needing to break a sweat. My dalliance with the Middle East took time, but at least things were always moving forward, regardless of how slowly. Overall then, our problems in Malaysia represent the first blow to our expansion plans, but it is far from a fatal one. And as the saying goes, whatever doesn't kill you makes you stronger. That's for damn sure.

That fateful night in July 2011. Having dinner with Anders and Jimmy, and ultimately deciding to open a bakery together. Sometimes you must listen to your gut feel. Cheers to that!

Planning began immediately, often in planes or cafés on the other side of the world, with scribblings on napkins and notebooks, which were shot and sent to the designers. This is how many great ideas became reality.

I remember sitting on a plane scribbling out our vision and mission statement. I still carry these with me in my backpack. They form the very essence of what I believe in and what I want Baker & Cook to stand for. There is a reason they are in black and white. Today, the vision statement sits proudly in each and every store to remind myself and my team of why we do what we do!

After a few months searching and being firmly focused on opening in suburban neighbourhoods, Anders found the perfect site at 77 Hillcrest Road (known as Greenwood), in Bukit Timah, Singapore. We signed the lease in September 2011.

On the many occasions I would fly in from Copenhagen, Denmark, on my way to New Zealand for a week of meetings, discussions and planning. I remember thinking, "Surely I can just cut down that no entry sign!" How wrong was I?

With the hoarding up, we started to burn cash. Let the games begin with the contractors and designers!

One of the many, many meetings with the contractors and designers just to keep them on track. Having gone through this experience, I am never shocked anymore regarding their logic, or lack of it!

Discussing the nightclub-style darkened windows that had to be removed and replaced.

It cost us an additional $200,000 to redo the roof and drainage — all the hidden costs of production. It was a lot of money at that time!

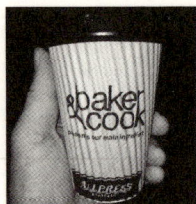

The day before our official opening, we had a special visitor to wish us well and welcome us to their neighbourhood. It was President Tony Tan Keng Yam and Mrs Mary Tan. They live a short distance away from our flagship store in Hillcrest Road and are now regular customers.

We were the first in the world to co-brand with Allpress Coffee. It made sense to me, given that we wanted people to know we were serious about coffee. The Antipodeans loved it!

Baker & Cook's flagship neighbourhood store at 77 Hillcrest Road was a fresh approach to an artisan bakery and food store. My vision was to have a place where people could come and hang out at any time of the day within their own neighbourhood.

The simple, clean lines of the display counters are key for me. A bakery is all about the food. You must be able to see the product. The food is the hero and the star of any bakery.

January 2012, before the clampdown. We had an additional 50 seats outside the Hillcrest Road store. The drop in weekly sales hit us hard, but we survived as we had created something special and we had loyal customers.

Before we set up our social media platform, when we lost our outdoor seating.

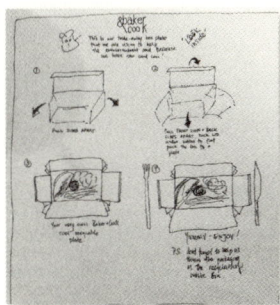

August 2012. After we recovered from the shock of having our outdoor seating taken away, we created a take-away box to work within the rules of not serving people on our premises. So if you ordered scrambled eggs, we placed it in this take-away box which could be converted into a plate according to the instructions on the lid. Despite this, the crowds didn't stop coming to our Hillcrest Road store.

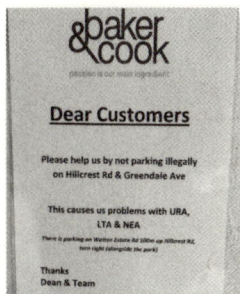

Our sign to let customers know where they can park when they visit our store.

This is one of my favourite photos. It embodies the very essence of what I wanted to achieve with Baker & Cook. The demand for freshly baked artisan bread spread like wild fire in Singapore. We became the talk of the town.

In 2015, we sold part of the business to Commonwealth Capital Pte Ltd and Atlantic Partners Ltd. Both companies loved the spirit, passion and vision Baker & Cook had developed, and they have become great partners. Their mandate was "keep doing what you do and we are here to support you." From left: myself, Andrew Kwan, Anders Boye and Anthony Stiefel.

May 2015. The media caught wind of what Baker & Cook was doing and we were praised for bringing greatness and culture to Singapore's neighbourhoods.

The flyer we distributed in the neighbourhood to announce our opening.

The easy and relaxed charm inside Plank Sourdough Pizza reflects the same casual, homey feeling projected by the recycled shutters that adorn the exterior.

May 2015. Plank Sourdough Pizza Swan Lake Avenue in its full glory!

Working with food blogger Dr Leslie Tay on our Pizza #7.

Plank Sourdough Pizza in full swing. Due to the rave reviews, people came from all over Singapore. Keeping things simple was key to Plank's success, plus not trying to be Italian, because I am not!

The side view of Plank Sourdough Pizza.

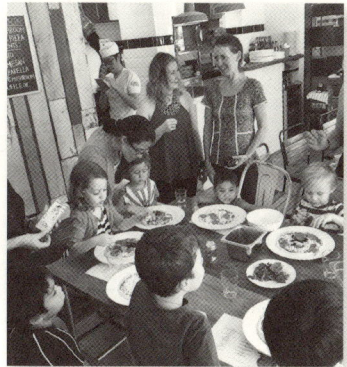

At Plank Sourdough Pizza, it's all about the community and families.

I still don't know what happened and what tipped one of my bakers over the edge one evening working on his own before everyone arrived at work. You can never tell what's happening in people's lives outside work. Never mind, we just cleaned it up and got on with things.

Vision Statement

To become the world's leading artisan bakery & foodstore brand, through adopting & delivering a "products we love" (PWL) and "service we love" (SWL) approach in everything we do.

We want to provide a modern, contemporary dining & shopping experience and will strive to enrich as many people's lives as possible with our passion, as our main ingredient, and pride.

Team members and customers are our lifeblood and at all times we will seek to exceed their expectations whilst sharing our ethos, "made by life" way.

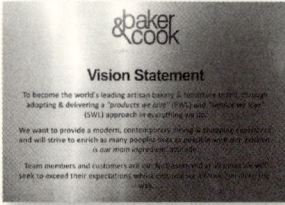

Our Vision Statement hangs in all our stores for both the staff and customers to read. Every now and then, if I think my staff are getting out of line, I remind them to read it.

Head office #1, from January 2012 to April 2015. Under the stairwell at 77 Hillcrest Road.

Head office #2, from April to October 2016. At 1 Greendale Avenue, Brettschneider's Baking & Cooking School.

Head office #3, from October 2016 to the present. At 1 Greendale Avenue, above Brettschneider's Baking & Cooking School.

The signboard ready to go up. There's no mistake! It's my Baking & Cooking School!

April 2016. Ready for business. Simple, clean and very welcoming. The school adds massive value to Baker & Cook and Plank Sourdough Pizza.

The school in its full glory with our key sponsors, Fisher & Paykel, Kenwood, Global Knives, SCANPAN and Silestone.

The school by night.

Out with the old and in with the new. Our shiny new SCANPAN cookware — we have a great group of sponsors for the school.

July 2016. A lovely welcome to The Bistro Group's head office for Anders and myself to begin the discussions for our first franchise in Manila, Philippines.

November 2016. Working with The Bistro Group's design and operations team for the opening of Baker & Cook and Plank Sourdough Pizza Manila. It was such a pleasure working with a well-organised, passionate and professional group.

The development of our international franchise was supported by IE Singapore. They helped us understand the markets we wanted to enter.

With my Singapore-based team during the pre-opening training in Manila. It was a great team effort and I'm very proud of my team.

January 2017. Who would have thought I would be on a 50-foot billboard hanging on the S Maison Mall in Manila announcing the opening of Baker & Cook?

11 January 2017. The ribbon-cutting ceremony with The Bistro Group's CEO, Jean-Paul Manuud (*left*), and other distinguished guests to celebrate the opening of Baker & Cook and Plank Sourdough Pizza Manila.

Mo & Jo Sourdough Burgers was born out of a desire to create a good, honest Antipodean burger made with sourdough buns. It also lets us extend the reach of Baker & Cook's pastry kitchen and continue our expansion across Singapore. Plus, we now have a scalable burger business.

I wanted an easy drinking beer to have with our pizzas and burgers. In 2018, Baker Boy Summer Ale was born.

We also launched a sliced artisan sourdough bread range in Singapore supermarkets to give more people access to great bread.

The Baker & Cook Group was named a 'Singapore SME 1000 Company' in 2018. I'm very proud that we have received this.

Baker & Cook at Al Khobar, Saudi Arabia, beside the InterContinental Hotel.

Adapting an overseas franchise: training the team in Saudi Arabia, and having products like this doughnut filled with rose-scented custard and decorated with rose petal icing and pistachios to suit local tastes.

Nine

Reflections

In most books of this type, this is usually the part where the successful entrepreneur puts his philosopher's hat on, dissects the nature of his business's success and outlines a step-by-step guide for the reader to follow in his daily life, planting him on a similar path to prosperity. Right. Well, it would take a special level of hubris to suggest that telling my story will change anyone's life. I'm not going to do that. But what I can offer are my reflections on a life spent in the baking business, the lessons learnt and the losses suffered. Take from it what you will — hopefully you'll find something useful.

If I reflect on my business journey first in terms of numbers — in typical Asian KPI style — then there's no question that things have worked out very well indeed. As I write this, I have 15 businesses in Singapore alone, counting Baker & Cook, Plank Sourdough Pizza, Mo & Jo Sourdough Burgers and Brettschneider's Baking and Cooking School. Looking forward, by the end of 2019, when all international franchises and joint ventures are added to the equation, then that number will become 22.

Sticking with numbers, I think it's obvious when I say my original stake of $200,000 as a founding partner has been paid back and then some, many times over, and I would expect a thriving business like Baker & Cook to command a pretty hefty fee were the business to ever be put on the market. It's always a bit classless to talk about money, but it's fair to say my sourdough has made me plenty of dough over the years. More figures: this book will be my 16th published book, with one more due before 2019 is done with. And 500,000 — that's the number of people in New Zealand who tuned in to watch *The Great Kiwi Bake Off* finale, for which I was the judge and will be again in season two in 2019.

All very impressive, right? But numbers alone cannot tell a full story. They're not meaningless; as broad indicators of my businesses' financial success, I take satisfaction from when I have time to dwell on them. But let me tell you, that isn't often. I dare say there aren't many successful business people in the world who spend all day staring at their company bio page, marvelling at all the past success they've had. They're too busy running those businesses to make sure they stay successful.

Let me give you two more numbers that help explain what I mean: 20 and $200. The first refers to the number of bagels a loyal customer wanted to order from us recently for a corporate lunch her company was hosting. But there was just one request she wished to make: our standard bagels were too big for her needs, so could we make them a little smaller for her instead? The order would have been worth $200. I say "would have been" because this poor customer had the misfortune of making her enquiry to one of the laziest and most brain-dead general managers I have ever come across. His reply was: "I'm sorry, our bagels only come in that standard size. Would you be interested in a different type of pastry instead?" She wasn't. Order lost and $200 went down the drain. The email exchange with the customer found its way to me, as they often do. I drove straight to the outlet where I knew the manager was working at the time.

I greeted him by asking, "Can you give me $200?"

"Ah, er, sorry sir, I don't think I know what you mean?"

"I would just like to have $200, and seeing as you think $200 is nothing, then I don't see why you can't just give it to me."

"I, uh, I don't have $200 right now but maybe, um, if —"

I stopped him there and then and told him what I was getting at. He was never to turn away ready business like that again. Did he think our bakers were spending 24 hours a day playing cards in the custom-built baking kitchen? No, they were baking stuff from scratch every bloody day and night. If a customer wants 20 bagels to be 30 per cent smaller, then you call the production manager and ask him to bake 20 bagels that are 30 per cent smaller. How difficult is that?

That general manager no longer works for us, by the way.

Sticking with the numbers game: 60 days. A pretty standard credit term for us with suppliers. I insist that my accountants stick to it. They are never to pay even a single day early. After one accountant broke this rule and paid a $340 vegetable invoice early, she felt my wrath. She said, "I don't understand. We have X million in the bank, and the bill was only $340. I thought I'd just pay it a few weeks early and get it out of the way."

"Right," I said, "but we might need that $340 for something before the invoice is due. You never know. And now the supplier will think of us as a soft touch. Wait and see. Now they'll start delivering to us late, or sending us crap produce."

What I'm getting at is that Baker & Cook climbed to become a big company by acting like a small one. I remind my staff all the time that we must continue to think of our business as the small, friendly neighbourhood bakery it started life as, the kind of business where every cent counts. We must stay sharp and humble and never ever think of ourselves as the kind of multi-outlet, multi-national company that doesn't mind turning away $200 orders, or the type to casually pay a $340 tomatoes bill early. It is only by continuing to worry about the small numbers that the big numbers will show up on the P&L statement.

No doubt the manager who turned away the bagels order thought, "Okay, I messed up, but why did Dean get so riled up? It was only one order." I have heard variations of this refrain on countless similar occasions from friends, bosses, partners and staff all throughout my life. If forced to answer, I say it comes down to passion. But even then, that word 'passion' doesn't totally encapsulate what I mean. I need a word that combines passion with drive, determination, obsession and commitment. Whatever the right word is, I'm talking about the 'I am going to conquer this challenge at all costs' mentality that I have. It's the crux of everything, really.

And I mean that seriously. I am not talking about passion in the 'I'm a passionate foodie!' sense I see in CVs from prospective new employees all the time. I didn't get to where I am because I quite like baking and have a bit of a knack for it. I have gotten to where I am by recognising a talent early and thereafter pouring sweat and blood into it for more than 30 years, living baking and breathing it. I make it a point to impress this upon those hopeful new youngsters who are earnestly pleading for a job.

I really want them to know what they're letting themselves in for. "50 to 60 working hours a week, blisters on your feet, sweltering kitchens, unsociable working hours and shit pay. This is what is coming, and I don't need you to just tolerate it, I need you to love it and then come back for more. Are you sure, and I mean really sure, that you are up for it?"

I think of passion — the true 'fuck sleeping or eating, there's work to be done' kind — as a characteristic, part of your genetic code. You either have it or you don't. It's not like learning a foreign language or taking up a musical instrument. It's not something you can teach yourself as you get older. To me, saying "I am passionate" is akin to saying "I am a New Zealander". It is just part of who I am, and I don't deserve any credit for being formed that way. That's how I define passion, and I suggest that any young person out there reading this makes damn well sure they possess that characteristic before even beginning to think about a career in the F&B business or life as an entrepreneur. Passion is no guarantor of success — far from it. There are plenty of passionate failures out there. But it is a prerequisite you must have before you even reach the starting line. Without it, there's no point even entering the race.

Still, characteristics alone will only take you so far. Talent, another prerequisite, is a tricky bastard to manage. First, you have to figure out what your talent is. Doing so isn't easy. And once you do that, you have to wrestle with that talent the rest of your life to wring the most you possibly can out of it. It was lucky, really, that I discovered a talent with my hands back as a kid in Waikuku Beach. Through sport and woodwork to begin with, and then home economics, which led me to baking. Some people might say this is a calling but I don't believe in that kind of mystical voodoo. I just look back and realise that baking was the perfect fit for me, my character and temperament, and even my physicality.

My early career experiences cemented the sense that I belonged in the baking world, from my apprenticeship with John van Til, the baking competitions, and my time rebounding around various kitchens in London, to the year spent at the Montagu Arms during my OE. I had early success in all of these endeavours, but none of it came easy. I can see now that the Apprentice of the Year title I earned as a teenager was critical. Having been given a taste of being on top, of being named number one in something, I was determined to meet that standard in whatever else I did thereafter.

And to be the best in whatever I did required constantly and consciously sharpening and developing my skills, which I did relentlessly. Every career change I made was strategic, invariably timed for precisely the moment I had felt I had learnt all I could from the previous position. My roles at Ernest Adams and teaching at the New Zealand Baking Training Centre topped up the technical knowledge I'd gained during my apprentice years, equipping me to run my first business, Windsor Cakes, successfully for three years. That was followed by an extended stint at Goodman Fielder, where I developed an international perspective towards both baking itself and, more importantly, the business of baking.

From Goodman Fielder to BakeMark in China and back to Lantmannen Unibake in Europe, further global connections were formed and business forays launched — all while a string of books were published and TV appearances made, which developed a public personal brand of Dean Brettschneider, the Baker Boy, the New Zealand Baker, the Global Baker.

When I list my career timeline out like that, it seems almost inevitable that Baker & Cook came next, taking root in 2012 and immediately flourishing. It was the logical culmination of an untroubled career ascent, the reward for a perfectly managed assembly of skills and experience that prepared me for the job of a lifetime. Of course, it wasn't quite like that. That's too neat a narrative and it ignores the digressions and distress that came along the way.

Broadly though, it is true to say that I always moved with an unerring sense of direction, that every step I took was one leading me to something better and bigger. I still have that feeling, that impulse propelling me forward. For me, the present-day Baker & Cook, 22 global businesses or not, is not the peak of the mountain. It can't be.

That feeling is a bittersweet one. It's the feeling that no matter what achievements are made, how many outlets are opened and how many millions in revenue are earned, it's still not enough. It is a feeling that means I can never stop to smell the roses. Sure, our business is strong, but why do I still drive by dozens of other bakeries every day and see customers in them? Why aren't they spending their money at Baker & Cook instead? Why were there two empty tables at the Serangoon Plank outlet when I checked in last night? Why did I spot a complaint on our baking school's Facebook page the other day? Why isn't everything perfect all of the time?

There is no on/off switch to this part of me, which I am aware makes me different from most people. You hear a lot of would-be entrepreneurs and business people talk about doing whatever necessary to become successful; they'll make it to the top at all costs. 99 per cent of the time when you hear this kind of thing, it's nothing but rhetoric, or just plain bullshit. What they really mean is, "I'm willing to work hard for a year or two, maybe work the odd 12-hour day. I'll even answer emails from home and check in on the business for an hour on Sunday afternoons." These kind of folks, bless their souls, will still take their days off for their kids' birthdays, or when their great aunt falls down the stairs. I'm sorry, but that's not enough.

When I told myself I would make Baker & Cook succeed at all costs, I meant it. Really meant it. The costs I've paid confront me every day, both emotionally and physically.

From a personal perspective, my relentless focus on the business was unquestionably a major factor in my split with my first wife. The hours were so long and the travel demands so intense. Even when we did have a few hours together, the pent-up exhaustion and stress made it difficult to put as much into the relationship as it deserved. This, sadly, was a pattern that repeated itself with my second wife, amongst other things, and our divorce was confirmed during the course of writing this book.

I lost countless hours from Jason's childhood. All that time spent in bakeries at 3 a.m. or on flights back and forth to China were hours that could otherwise have been spent assembling Lego together or throwing a rugby ball around. The pain of losing that time with him is at least softened by the fact we share such an awesome relationship now as he enters into adulthood.

Looking beyond my family, I'm surprised sometimes that I still have any friends left, given how often I've turned down their invitations to weddings, birthday parties, christenings or simple Friday nights down at the pub. Such everyday friendly camaraderie that so many take for granted is a precious commodity for someone like me.

Physically, it's fair to say that a lifetime of baking has taken a toll on my body. The ever-present aches and exhaustion I can live with — they come with the job. But things took a more serious turn a few years ago when I started experiencing excruciating pain in my lower back. A scan showed me I had a collapsed disc in my lower spine. A sensible person would have rested and managed it, as the doctor instructed me to do, but I kept working. What choice did I have?

A year later the disc ruptured and I ended up needing emergency surgery. It was bad — at one stage I was in danger of losing my bladder and bowel. Still, the surgery seemed to go well and I soon recovered enough to get back up on my feet, check myself out and pick up my mobile phone. Time to get back to work.

Another year passed — this was now mid-2018 — and the pain just got worse. I sought a second opinion and found out that the previous surgery had been the equivalent of putting a piece of sticky tape over a gaping wound. As it was, the surgeon said, my back would only hold together if I retired immediately and effectively stopped all form of physical activity for the rest of my life — hardly a realistic proposition.

The only alternative was to go back under the knife, which I did in October 2018. The procedure, in a final bid to keep my spine in one piece, involved screwing it back together with titanium. The doctors didn't mince their words beforehand; they made it clear that even with this intervention I would still feel pain and discomfort almost daily. They weren't wrong on that score. And as for how my back will feel in my later years? Well,

246 PASSION IS MY MAIN INGREDIENT

let's not think about that for now. As one of the physiotherapists pointed out to me during my long and painful rehab: I have literally broken my back for my business.

When I reflect on these emotional and physical costs, I can't help but ask myself, is it all worth it? I also wonder, should these be classed as sacrifices or selfishness? Neither, or both? I can't answer those questions. I can only say that like everyone else, life presented me with a never-ending series of decision points, which were very rarely binary, black or white, right or wrong options. I made my choices and at every juncture I tried to make the best one I could for everyone involved. It would be a fool's errand to look back now and imagine the innumerable permutations different decisions at different stages could have led to. The results are what they are and I'm reasonably comfortable with them.

All that remains to be asked is, "What's next?" Time will tell, but new opportunities present themselves from new and exciting angles on a practically daily basis now, both in a Baker & Cook context and beyond. There is no rush. I am sure a new direction will unveil itself when it is ready, a corner of the world bearing a challenge too tempting not to take on. Until then, there is the staffing issue to settle at the new outlet, the potential partner to visit in Delhi, the site to scout for in Riyadh, the radio interview to do, the proofs of my next book to check, the website rebuild to complete, the teaching class to prepare for, and every other one of a thousand things that make up a day in my business. A day in my life.

The price of business and passion — my collapsed and ruptured disc resulted in a need for titanium implant supports and screws to fuse my vertebrae together.

I'm a firm believer in sticking to one's knitting — baking being my knitting. But I've discovered that there is more to being a good baker than just making a good pastry, cake or loaf of bread. Would I do any of it again? In a heartbeat. I don't believed in luck; instead, I believe life's challenges and making choices with the attitude of 'if something is meant to be, it's up to me'.

Winning Expatpreneur of the Year in 2019 (awarded by SPH Magazines' *The Finder*) is a huge honour. I am extremely proud of my team of the past and present because this award is truly for them.

What lies ahead? I'm not sure, but for the first 50 years of my life, I've enjoyed the ride. I've had fun, met amazing people and done incredible things, realising through it all that passion is my main ingredient.

About the Author

Dean Brettschneider is one part professional baker and one part entrepreneur. Arguably one of the world's best bakers with an international following, Dean is truly a global baker. He resides in Singapore, where he heads up his global baking empire. He travels regularly to all corners of the world as a consultant to the global F&B and baking industry. He is the founder and co-owner of the global artisan bakery and food store chain Baker & Cook, Plank Sourdough Pizza, Mo & Jo Sourdough Burgers, and Brettschneider's Baking & Cooking School, and also co-owner of the London-based Crosstown Doughnuts. An author of 16 award-winning books on baking, Dean is also a judge on successful reality TV series such as *New Zealand's Hottest Home Baker* and *The Great Kiwi Bake Off*. He also hosts the *Kiwi Baker* series in Shanghai, France, Singapore and California, as well as many other TV programmes that promote baking excellence, travel, food and culture. For more information, see www.globalbaker.com